The Liberated Heart

*Moving From Rules and Control
to Relationships of the Heart*

Valerie Acuff

ISBN 978-1-936944-00-2

First Printing 2011

Library of Congress Number 2011932509.

Published by Daystar Rising L.L.C.

4

Dedicated to:

My children,
Todd and Heather

My greatest regret is sacrificing your childhood to the rules of a controlling belief system. If I could change anything in my life, it would be this!

About the Author

Valerie Acuff attended the University of Pennsylvania majoring in psychology. She worked in the Department of Psychology of U of P and continued her studies in this field over the years.

She has developed and presented programs, retreats, workshops and seminars on personal growth, relationship issues and spiritual development internationally in the United States, England, France, Africa, Northern Ireland, New Zealand and Australia. She has also made guest appearances on radio and TV in the United States, England and Australia discussing relationship issues and responding to listeners' questions.

She and her late husband, Walt, shared a counseling practice in addition to her overseeing a program for the prevention of domestic abuse. While she travels extensively, Valerie makes her home in England.

This book is an edited version of a 5-night series of talks given in 1995 in Colorado Springs, Colorado under the title "From Legalism to Love". Valerie was involved with Jehovah's

Witnesses from September, 1960 until June, 1984 when she found the courage to walk away during a summer convention and in leaving, found the freedom to follow her life's calling of writing, speaking and teaching.

Acknowledgements

Many people have encouraged me to write about this subject and it is now my opportunity to let them know how much I appreciate them.

First and foremost are my children who have become my friends as they've moved into adulthood. Hopefully, they have forgiven me for raising them with painful memories of all they could not participate in because of my belonging to this organization. I am very proud of you both and grateful for your loving me in spite of the past.

Next are my dear friends, past and present, who are now enjoying freedom after leaving controlling belief systems. You are too numerous to name but you know who you are. The bond of sharing this experience and finding the courage to discover your own life's path will be forever strong.

Thanks especially go to Linda Schauer who encouraged me on a daily basis to take pen to paper, to Gillie Buck who picked me up when I was down and has been my champion, to Cynthia Manner who proofread every page and prodded me to keep going, to Barbara Radke who inspired and encouraged me with her questions and realizations and to Barbara Foote who is my friend, neighbor and Personal Assistant. These women are truly sisters in my heart.

Finally, my never ending gratitude to my late husband, Walt, who was my best friend, the dearest husband possible and an amazing man with the biggest heart I've encountered in this lifetime.

Do well to all you meet, and if you cannot do good at least do no harm.

The Dalai Lama

The Liberated Heart

This is a typed and edited transcript of a four night series of talks called "Legalism to Love" given in Colorado Springs, CO, USA in 1995 by Valerie Acuff. Because this is a transcript of a talk, the written flow may not always appear smooth but does retain the integrity of the original message.

When I was first asked to talk with you and share my background as one of Jehovah's Witnesses in the Watchtower in a nightly series for this week, I thought, "That's not a problem." I've spoken on this a lot in the past. In fact, years ago, I spoke publicly on a fairly regular basis, but I hadn't visited my memories of that world for a long time. So it was like looking back to a time I had forgotten I once lived through.

I agreed to speak on this subject because most people are unaware of the emotional and spiritual torment suffered by Jehovah's Witnesses. In fact, Jehovah's Witnesses themselves are unaware of it. It is only after one wakes up and realizes the seriousness of their own personal situation and leaves that they become aware of the difficulty they have to function as an independent person outside of that organization. People in general, and ex-Witnesses in particular, have no idea of the damage done to themselves and their children, the struggle to get out, and the work needed to rebuild themselves emotionally in order to build a happy and healthy life.

When you are talking to people who were in cults (or any kind of controlling relationship) and you ask them to look back to the time before they came into the cult or the relationship, you're asking them to look at a world they may have forgotten existed. There are so many different approaches I could use to share about my own personal history. But this evening I wanted to talk about how I got involved, what coerced me to stay and what helped me to leave.

I got involved in the way that most people slowly become involved with Jehovah's Witnesses. But I want to stress that what I am about to share isn't just about the kind of organization or church that you might label a cult. What I will be talking about is what happens to anyone who gets caught up in any controlling relationship whether it is with an individual or an organization. The process is the same. There are challenges going into that kind of relationship, but there are even bigger challenges coming out. And we will talk about those also as this week progresses.

I was in the Watchtower, you know those people who ring your doorbell at the most inconvenient times. I was in that organization for 24 years and for part of that time I was a full time worker for them. I had received specialized training from them at their school for people in leadership. Women are not in a position of leadership, but I was married to a Congregation Overseer who had formerly worked at the Watchtower Headquarters in Brooklyn, New York. We were what were called 'Special Pioneers' and so in that capacity I was invited to attend. I'll go more into what that term 'Special Pioneer' means later on.

Tonight, I will *not* be sharing with you negative messages about the Watchtower organization, nor will I be giving you pointers on how to argue with them at the door. I have moved my life in a positive direction and am not interested in sharing a negative message. But I do want to share with you what goes on in the life of the person who is ringing your doorbell so you can know this is a person who really has a heart for God but has been seriously misled. The person ringing your doorbell is not your enemy. The person at your door is a victim. They are victims of a very insidious process.

To give you some of my personal background, I was raised as a Christian and grew up in the church. I was born and spent my early years in England and there my family belonged to the Salvation Army. In England, the Salvation Army is more of a church than a charity as it is regarded in the United States. I grew up during World War II and my father was in the Royal Air Force so he was gone for the first five years of my life. It was just my mother and I. She was one of the Local Officers in the Salvation Army, which is similar to a lay preacher, so we practically lived at the church. We were there Sunday morning, afternoon and evening and a couple of evenings in the week. I can never remember a time when the church wasn't a big part of my life. I just can't remember a time that wasn't true for me.

In fact, my mother taught me to read before I started school and she used the Bible to do that. By the time I was five years old I could even read through some of the 'begats'. You know, 'so and so' begat 'so and so'. It came easily to me and I learned the stories of the Bible in that process from a very early age.

About a year or so after we came to the United States, when I was about nine years old, my parents started going to a Baptist church and on Easter Sunday morning just before I was 11 years old I was baptized.

After I graduated high school at age 16, I worked full time while attending the University of Pennsylvania. My goal was to become a medical missionary at the Baptist Hospital in what was then called Leopoldville, Africa. Today that area is known as Kinshasa in Zaire. I studied psychology and medicine because those were the pre-requisite courses I needed to accomplish my goal.

The church I belonged to during this time was in West Philadelphia and was what you would call a 'tight-knit' church. It was small, people knew each other, people were involved in each other's lives and everyone felt a close connection. It was a very warm and friendly church.

However, in the late 1950's the neighborhood the church was in began to change and the elders of that church took a vote. They did a terrible thing in my eyes and the eyes of my family. They voted that they would only accept white people. They would baptize anyone who requested it, but would only accept whites for church membership. So my family left the church because that decision was not tolerable for us. We then struggled to find another church home. We visited several others and went to one for a year or so but we never had that same feeling again. It just wasn't quite there.

My father had studied on and off with Jehovah's Witnesses for years. We always had some Watchtowers or Awake magazines in the bathroom because that's where a lot of reading got done. I was used to seeing it there, stacked on top of the clothes hamper.

Finally when I was 20 and no longer living at home, my mother invited me to come to their home for a study she and my Dad had been having with Jehovah's Witnesses. They had been studying with them in their home every Thursday evening for about a year. My mother asked me to come and prove them wrong.

I did sit in on their study that night. Right now I'm going to put this overhead on and keep it up on the screen, because I'm going to show you the progression of what I call, "The Wedge of Involvement". It's how I got caught up in it that night and how everyone in a controlling relationship or group gets caught up and realizes too late how hard it is to get out.

THE WEDGE OF INVOLVEMENT

STAGES	ACTIVITY
1	• Discussion
2	• Interest • Hope • 'The Truth'
3	• Friendliness • Feel loved • Belonging • 'Family' feeling • Fellowship • Participation
4	• Meetings • Preparation • Study • 'Right' answers • Work / Give your time
5	• Special Teachings • Separation from friends & family • Cultural isolation • Rules • We/They thinking • Uniformity of beliefs • Loss of individualism
6	• Detailed accountability • Spying • Lack of personal authority • Lack of Joy • Life on 'hold'
7	• Trapped • No one to turn to • Weariness • Fear of losing family, friends and eternity

Stage 1 – The Discussion

Jehovah's Witnesses know the Bible well and really know how to move easily through it. How many of you have talked to one of them and felt so frustrated when you were done you couldn't believe it? I mean, you just want to stop the conversation and say, "Don't you get it?" because it's back and forth, back and forth and moving from one verse to another. But, if you listen to what they say, it does sound very appealing.

Initially what they shared with me that night was very appealing and did make sense because of the way they presented it. In any new relationship, whether with a person or a group, it always looks good in the first stages. They caught my interest. They shared their hope for the future and presented it as the 'truth' of scripture. To me it seemed like something that had been hidden in the words of scripture that was suddenly revealed and now made sense.

They invited me to come that weekend to one of their small assemblies where about 2,000 people gathered together twice a year. I'm not sure what happens today. Jehovah's Witnesses congregations at that time were divided into what was called circuits. There were between 15 to 20 congregations in a circuit, which meant each circuit had about 2,000 people.

Twice a year they would have what is called a 'Circuit Assembly' and all those congregations would come together for three days. So I went to one of those in Philadelphia. There was such a family feeling of warmth and togetherness that I thought these people must have something. These people are onto something.

Stage 2 – Interest / Hope / The "Truth"

During your first discussion Witnesses talk about things that interest you, such as having healthy children, happiness in your relationships and peace on the earth. They then go on to talk about the hope of a life without illness or pain and they will credit you with particular insight for recognizing 'The Truth'.

Interest

Witnesses talk about things that sound really good and show you scriptures to back up what they are telling you. Of course, the scriptures are out of context. But when you are hungry for something and wanting to belong somewhere and you're feeling a bit left out, it sounds wonderful. It really does sound wonderful! This is true of all cults. This is how all the cults work. It's how all-controlling relationships start.

Hope

There is a feeling of hope for the future and you believe it's what you've been looking for. You want to believe the future is bright and that your children will grow up in a better world than you've experienced. You want to see a world without sickness, debts, hunger, disease or death. They hold out the hope of living on this planet in ultimate peace and harmony forever, but it is a hope held out to only the few who believe them and become part of what they are working for.

The 'Truth'

You want to believe them because they say they have 'the truth'. That's the mark of a cult. It is also the mark of a congregation in any church denomination that may be moving in that direction. And you've seen that happen in some churches when they say, "Our church has 'The Truth'" or "Our church is the 'right' one".

One of the big questions that Jehovah's Witnesses will ask you is, "If you were alive when Noah built his ark, would you have gotten onto the ark?" That would make you think, wouldn't it? Then they tell you that this is the ark. This is it! This is the ark today! The Watchtower Bible and Tract Society is the ark. And you don't want to be left out when the door shuts do you? So you want to know more and more.

Stage 3 – Friendliness / Feel Loved / Belonging / 'Family' Feeling / Fellowship / Participation

Friendliness / Feel Loved / Belonging

At this stage you're getting more and more into this warm family, a feeling of belonging, or at least wanting to belong to such a loving group, and there is a lot of fellowship. You see, what happens when you come to a Kingdom Hall, someone will invite you to a barbecue or a picnic or some other event in someone's home. There's always something going on like a baby shower or a gathering of some sort at someone's house, or there will be something else happening. There is a lot of camaraderie. Once you begin studying with one of Jehovah's Witnesses then you are the one everyone wants to 'bring along' to help and encourage. So there is a lot of interest shown in you.

'Family' Feeling / Fellowship

When you first begin to study with them and you are invited to the Kingdom Hall, which is what they call their meeting places, you are impressed with the closeness everyone feels for each other. There is a camaraderie that is enviable. It is like a large extended family where everyone helps with each other's children, and seems to know each other extremely well.

If you are studying with them and especially if you are attending the meetings and, as an example, you are going to move from your house, you'll have 10 men and 6 trucks at your door on Saturday morning volunteering to help you, just like that. Where else in the world can you have an instant family who is that willing to help and to 'be there' for you?

How many of you have Jehovah's Witnesses in your families or how many of you are Jehovah's Witnesses sitting here listening to this? (Someone in the audience speaks). Okay. Are you studying with them? Have you been involved with them? (The person says "All my life"). Well I'm glad you're here because we are talking about very sincere people. We are talking about people with a wonderful heart for others. This is not about the people. It's about what's taught and what hurts. And it's about what is confusing as you move further and further into this. Thank you for coming tonight. I'm really glad you're here.

Participation

What happens next in stage three is your participation. You get brought into the activity and the work. I was in Philadelphia at the time I first got involved. But what happened there is typical of what happens around the world at a Kingdom Hall. At first you are invited to answer questions at the weekly studies and then you are invited to go door-to-door with someone else who will teach you by example and then train you. All of which moves us to stage four.

Stage 4 – Meetings / Preparation / Study / The 'Right' Answers / Work / Give Time

Meetings

What kind of involvement am I talking about with meetings, studies and work? To begin with on Sundays there are two meetings. There is a Watchtower study, which lasts for an hour, and which will come before or after a one-hour talk on a topic from the Bible. The Watchtower study will be based on a particular article in the magazine. The date that article is to be studied is printed on the back of the magazine. The article will have questions at the bottom of the page corresponding to the numbered paragraphs on that page. One of the men in a position of oversight in the congregation will conduct the study. He will ask the questions, then those seated in the hall will raise their hands and wait to be called on. After several people have been called on, the paragraph will be read. This will continue for an hour.

After that study there will be a song where people can stand to sing. The songs are pre-selected and listed also. If there is a piano and someone can play it, there will be music to guide the singing. If there is no piano or pianist, the congregation may play recorded music accompaniment purchased from the Watchtower. If these are not available then the singing will be without any musical help. After the song another man will deliver a talk based on a sermon outline provided by the Watchtower Headquarters and he will speak for one hour. Only men do the speaking and teaching. There is no question and answer time after the one-hour talk.

There isn't a nursery for the children. Everybody sits together. Children are taught to sit still and cannot walk around or make any noise for the two hours. If the children fidget they are taken to the back or outside for discipline. Usually they will fall asleep. We used to have a saying that Jehovah's Witness kids could sleep on a straight-backed chair and my kids learned how to do that because they were raised in this.

These are the two hours of meeting on Sunday. There is also an hour on Tuesday night, which is a weekly Bible study. This is usually 8 to 10 people and may be limited to a maximum of 15 depending on the size of the congregations. This is similar to a 'cell group' and they will meet together every week. This same group will usually work together going door-to-door.

On Thursday evening, there is another two-hour meeting. The first hour is called the Theocratic Ministry School. There are five people assigned to give a specific talk for a specific length of time on a specific subject. Then they will be graded. There is a sheet that walks speakers through points that are being worked on, such as whether you were clear and understandable, how was your diction, how did you apply the scriptures and other topics. So they bring you along and train you on how to speak door-to-door in this way. Women participate by speaking to another woman or a child to simulate a discussion and avoid the appearance of a woman teaching the congregation.

The hour following the Theocratic Ministry School is designed to further teach and train people to speak door-to-door. There are specific sermon outlines. When a Witness comes to your door with a sermon, it is rehearsed. They know what they are going to say to you. It is the same sermon used all over the United States. Other countries are about six months behind on average because of the translation. We used to visit friends in Mexico and would sometimes attend the meetings there so we would see that the studies and the door-to-door work were about six months behind what was going on in the US.

Preparation / Study

All of those meetings have to be prepared for and in addition, you are out in 'field service' (going door-to-door) two to three hours a week. When I was involved, the recommendation for field service was 10 hours a month, but I'm not sure if they are as strict as they were when I was in it. I've been out since 1984 but they were fairly strong in recommending this number of hours per month in the sixties and seventies.

As I've said before, there is a strong 'family feeling' in the congregation. These people do love each other, they care for each other and they are there for each other. This is about people who are very kind-hearted. It is about people who have a deep love for God and who are searching for truth. The reason someone is in the Watchtower is that they do love God. They do want to know what God's word says. But they receive a misleading teaching.

The feelings of love and belonging are very strong, so strong that you can't think of leaving. You are encouraged to leave what they call 'worldly friends'. They quote First Corinthians 15:33 as a real watchword scripture, which says, "Bad association spoils useful habits" in their New World Translation. You've all heard they have their own Bible. Have you heard that? It's actually printed by the Watchtower Bible and Tract Society. It's called the New World Translation of the Holy Scriptures.

The 'Right' Answers

I had my translation of that Bible bound in black leather. In the back, after the concordance (which is usually included at the end of the Bible) I had another book called "Make Sure of All Things Hold Fast To What Is True" bound right in with that version of the Bible. This book is a topical concordance put out by the Watchtower that gives short sermons on specific issues. So if something were to come up at the door that I didn't know from the top of my head I could turn to this and begin to read from it and to point the householder to the scriptures from this book. It looks to the person who answered the door like you're reading from the Bible because it is printed on the same kind of paper and is bound right in it at the end. Many, many Witnesses had this inserted into their Bibles for the same reason I did.

If you were to write to any other Bible translating companies and ask them who were the scholars that translated their Bible, they would send you back a letter saying who those translators were, give you their credentials and their background. If you write to the Watchtower and ask who are the scholars who translated their Bible, they may not answer your letter. But if they do, they will not give you any names or further information.

I happen to have met some of the translators because of the position my first husband had in their headquarters and because of some of the work we did afterwards. One of the translators was Fred Franz and at that time he was the Vice President of the Watchtower. He had two years of Greek at the University of Cincinnati. Another one of the translators was Albert Schroeder. He is a brilliant man. I got to know him during our specialized training and he is very intelligent. He is self-taught in Greek and Hebrew and I understood he could speak both Biblical Greek and Hebrew. However, so far as I know, he didn't have degrees in either of these languages. Another was George Ganges who speaks modern day Greek. But none of the other translators spoke or understood Hebrew or Greek to my knowledge. Nor, so far as I know, did they have degrees in either of those languages.

What it appears the translating team actually did, was to go through other English translations and then collectively look at scriptures that they just changed slightly to reflect the message they wanted to get across. They say that they went back to the 'Ben Asher Texts' for the Hebrew and 'Westcott and Hort' for the Greek. In reality, it appears they may or may not have gone to either of those sources, but they did go to other English translations and put in subtle changes.

Work / Give Your Time

As you move through this process you are slowly moving into this controlling organization. It is a gradual process. The Watchtower Bible and Tract Society is not something you join. You don't 'join' Jehovah's Witnesses. This is something that you study and slowly, over time, become a part of. And so next you are invited to participate in the work.

The work is going door-to-door. At first you will work with someone and you will learn how to speak door-to-door and learn how to deal with what comes up and the kind of treatment you receive from householders. In most of the congregations we were in I was one of the people new ones would go out with and I would work with them and train them. We frequently worked in congregations that were identified as 'where the need is great'. This is the phrase that was used that meant they needed some help.

At the age of 22 I married a young man who worked at the Society's headquarters in Brooklyn, New York. Nathan Knorr was the president of the Society at that time. Prior to our getting married, my husband worked in this office for a while and then later in the office of the Treasurer. Jehovah's Witnesses are controlled by what they call a Governing Body. Today there are about 19 men on the Governing Body. At that time, in the early 60's, there were about nine or ten men and we knew who they were. Some we knew better than others. When we announced our engagement in 1962 at the Brooklyn headquarters they had a small reception for us. Most of those people were there to congratulate us. So I had married someone who was closely involved with the inner circle of what was going on. The headquarters in Brooklyn, New York is called Bethel, which means 'house of God'.

The people who work at Bethel are there by special invitation. While there they are assigned jobs and given room and board. They are working from 8 a.m. until 6 p.m. Monday through Friday and on Saturday from 8 a.m. until noon. They are all assigned to congregations in the New York area and are expected to attend all the meetings and go door-to-door on Saturday afternoon and Sunday morning with the members of the congregation.

At the time my husband was working there he received $14.00 a month allowance from the Watchtower Society, which was to cover incidentals such as toiletries and fares for public transportation to his congregation. If these young men and women didn't get financial help from their families or their congregations they struggle for even basic necessities such as toothpaste or bus fare. Those who had been there for many years received no pensions or Social Security and have no children to help them in their old age.

My husband left Bethel when we got married late in 1962 and we were sent out as what was called 'Special Pioneers' to Escanaba, Michigan. Special Pioneers are people who are required to put in 150 hours per month going door-to-door. Think about that. Every month, regardless of the weather or our health, we had to spend 150 hours knocking on doors. We had to conduct, each of us, individually, seven Bible studies a week with people in the community. That meant we each had to start a Bible study in seven separate homes. He had to have seven and I had to have seven. We could go on them together but there was a minimum that we had to be responsible for. We had to place a minimum of 10 books a month each going door-to-door. It was said that we 'placed' books and magazines. It was never said that we 'sold' them. We also had to 'place' 50 magazine each a month at the door.

We were not permitted to have any outside part time or full time work because the leaders of the Watchtower organization said it would detract from that service. When we received the letter telling us we were being sent to a place called Escanaba, Michigan I had to look it up on the map. Before this, I didn't know Michigan had an upper peninsula. I found out it's the place where they have nine months of good skiing weather and three months of bad. We lived in what was called locally, the 'banana belt' because in July we had a couple of weeks of summer.

It's a beautiful place. It really is beautiful. But we were sent up there to work with a congregation that we were told needed help. My husband was what the Watchtower called a 'Congregation Overseer', which is much like a pastor. So he had the work of overseeing everything and being available for people and leadership meetings in addition to the quotas that had to be met. If we each met these quotas of 150 hours per month, 7 Bible studies, 10 books, and 50 magazines each then we each got an allowance of $50 dollars that month to live on. Even in the sixties our combined amount of $100 a month was not much to live on and it didn't go far.

A married couple at that time was conservatively eating on about $20 to $25 a week. We could only budget $7.50 a week for groceries for the two of us. In addition we paid $15 a month to the Kingdom Hall for the privilege of living in a small room, approximately 125 square feet that was originally designed to be a book room.   Because we lived in the Kingdom Hall there was no hot running water and we used the men's and ladies rooms for our bathroom facilities.   We had a propane stove and a drop leaf table in one corner that we called a kitchen.   Once or twice a week we would go to someone's house for a shower and they would supply us with shampoo and conditioner because we couldn't afford them.

I stretched our food money by talking with the Produce Manager at our local supermarket and he held back the better 'day old' fruit and vegetables that were ready to be thrown out for me.   There was high unemployment at that time and a lot of people in that community were on what was at that time called, 'Aid to Dependent Children'.   It was a government program that gave food to families each month.   The food was very good quality and each family received more than they could use.   So often people traded food for books or magazines at the door.

I learned about fifty ways to prepare the canned meat, similar to spam, we would get.   I also learned how to bake bread because we got a lot of flour.   So all our cakes and pies were made from scratch with fruit from people's trees.   Once we were given a chicken that the householder traded for a book. She wrung its neck on the spot and we took home a fully feathered bird that this city girl had to pluck and gut (in a kitchen that had no running water) before cooking.

This was during the time that S&H Green Stamps were very popular. Most of you sitting here tonight probably never heard of them. But people would save these green stamps that were given out at grocery stores and gas stations to get household items such as dishes, glasses or toasters. People traded pages of these stamps with us for books and magazines and so our toaster, mixing bowls and even a hand cranked meat grinder were purchased with these stamps from the local redemption center.

I found that our circumstances made me extremely resourceful and I learned how to cook creatively using only the things we could afford or we traded for. Those lessons have served me well and for many years I baked all our bread and pastries and continued to hand grind our meat for meatloaf or hamburgers using what was available.

Most of our allowance went into our car for gas because we had a lot of territory to cover in the door-to-door work. It covered over 100 miles in one direction and we had to go door-to-door and cover all this territory in farming areas. I found out there was something more dangerous than a watchdog. People up there had geese. They are very mean and nasty creatures. They would squawk and bite, so when I saw geese, I marked that house as a 'not home'. I didn't enjoy encounters with geese!

We lived on the Upper Peninsula under those conditions and on that allowance for almost two years until we got pregnant with our first child, our son Todd. But while we were there doing that work, we were invited to go to what was then called Kingdom Ministry School. At that time it was held in upstate New York. It was a four-week training course just for Congregation Overseers and Special Pioneers. They held these courses 10 times a year. There was a week of work and then four weeks of school, a week of work and then again four of school and so on.

They would bring in about 100 people at a time. They would bring 100 men 10 times a year and only about 10 to 15 women in an entire year. The only women who came in were special pioneers and I was one of those women.

We were there for a total of five week, a week of work preparing for the incoming class and our four weeks of training. It's a very intensive work/training program. Even our class days were divided between working in the morning, classes in the afternoon and lectures in the evening. This schedule went Monday through Friday and Saturday morning.

The men who attended were not expected to make their beds, hang up their towels or clean their rooms. However, we women were expected to do that for ourselves on our own time and clean the rooms for the men as part of our work. We were all assigned tasks as it was a working farm providing the food for the school and Bethel in Brooklyn, which at that time was over 1500 people. My job was to clean quite a few of the men's rooms each day and work in the laundry folding towels and ironing shirts.

The men who attended had their personal laundry, including their shirts, done for them but the ladies attending had to do their own on their own time. We also had to participate in a local congregation going door-to-door and attending Sunday meetings where we were expected to have prepared and be ready to answer questions during the Watchtower study. During this time I learned a lot about the inner workings of the organization and how to defend their teachings. I also lost over 10 pounds during those five weeks. At five foot five inches I left weighing 104 pounds.

Stage 5 – Special Teachings / Separation From Friends and Family / Cultural Isolation / Rules / We/They Thinking / Uniformity of Beliefs / Loss of Individualism

I said earlier that I wasn't going to go into how to refute Jehovah's Witnesses and I'm not going to do that. However, I have been told that you are interested in knowing what some of the teachings are that differ from the mainstream and that can so isolate such a large group of people from their families, former friends and their community.

Special Teachings

When these people come to your door they are using the same terminology you do. So, you may ask, what is it that's different and why do they provide such intensive training for people in leadership? Basically, the first and foremost teaching is that God's name is to be used at all times and they say God's name is

Jehovah. They rarely, if ever, refer to God as 'God' but always as 'Jehovah', always by that personal name. They believe that God will only hear and honor your prayer if it is directed to him in His name, the name of Jehovah.

They also believe that when you die your soul will sleep - that your physical body is your soul. They teach that your body is your soul and when you die you will sleep until you are resurrected. Then this body, which is you, will be reconstructed, so you will be you again. But there is some controversy about how can you be you again if you have decayed. So you can see there is a problem here.

They also teach there is no hell fire and that hell is the grave.

They teach Jesus is not God, but he is Michael the Archangel, he came to the earth as Jesus and when he died, he was not bodily resurrected. They teach his body was dissipated into gases, was resurrected in spirit form, that he is in the heavens, began ruling in 1914 and is actually Michael the Archangel again. They refer to him as Jesus but they teach that he is Michael.

They believe that only 144,000 will go to heaven and that the rest of mankind will live on the earth forever. They believe those 144,000 are all Jehovah's Witnesses. They also believe only Witnesses will survive this coming cataclysm called Armageddon and if you are not baptized according to the Watchtower teachings you won't survive. Whether you have been baptized in a church or not you are to be re-baptized when you study with the Witnesses. Their baptism is in the name of the Father, the Son, and the Spirit begotten organization.

Jehovah's Witnesses believe that Jesus returned invisibly in 1914. Prior to that they taught he would bring his kingdom to power in 1875 and when nothing happened that year the date was changed to 1914. But what they originally taught about 1914 is pretty interesting. The original teaching was, that in 1914 the earth as we know it would end and as I said earlier, that would be the time for the cataclysm called Armageddon to come. In 1914, they said it would happen in the autumn of that year. The autumn came and went. The teaching was then changed to say that actually He's ruling invisibly in the heavens. They said Jesus is ruling invisibly in the heavens and we see him through the eyes of understanding.

To give you an idea of how they explain things like this, in 1918 there was a publication called, "Millions Now Living Will Never Die." On page 89 it says, *"Therefore we may confidently expect that 1925 will mark the return of Abraham, Isaac, Jacob and the faithful prophets of old, particularly those named by Paul in Hebrews 11, to the condition of human perfection."*

This belief was held so strongly they built a home in San Diego called "Beth Sarim", which means the House of Princes. It was deeded to Abraham, Isaac and Jacob awaiting their resurrection. The house still stands today and the deed is still recorded although it has been sold since. Most Witnesses today don't know about this house or what it was for. It's a beautiful home sitting on a hilltop with a beautiful view in a suburb of San Diego.

A person by the name of Judge Rutherford, the then president of the Watchtower Society, would live in it from time to time since Abraham wasn't using it yet. He would leave New York and enjoy the San Diego sunshine. When these prophets weren't resurrected and didn't appear in 1925, the

Watchtower in January 1, 1925 said, *"There was a lot of anticipation of this event."* This is a quote, *"The year 1925 is here. With great expectations Christians have looked forward to this year. Many have confidently expected that all members of the body of Christ will be changed to heavenly glory during this year. This may be accomplished. It may not be. In His own due time God will accomplish His purposes concerning his people."*

But the push and implication was there. That summer at the assemblies (and, I must add, 1925 was before my time) but from talking with people I knew who had been there at the time they said the anticipation that summer was just incredible. People were actually looking around the stadiums at assemblies, looking for Abraham, Isaac and Jacob. Every older man with a gray beard was looked at intently. They were so convinced these patriarchs would appear because of what they had been told.

In 1926, here is what the Watchtower said. *"Some anticipated that the work would end in 1925, but the Lord did not state so. The difficulty was the friends inflated their imaginations beyond reason. And when their imagination burst asunder they were inclined to throw away everything."* You might say that the leadership said it was going to happen in 1925 and when it didn't they blamed it on people getting too excited. We weren't there so who really knows.

However, I was there for their prophecies of 1975. In 1966, the anticipation began for 1975. The Watchtower began to say that 1975 would mark the end of six thousand years of human history because of the way they had counted chronologically through scripture. The information kept building and building. When the Circuit Servants would come into the congregations, which was twice a year, it would be a special time with special talks, especially on this subject of 1975. And then when the circuit assembly would be held it would again be a highly anticipated time of more talks on this subject.

Speakers at these events were saying things like, "Between 1966 and 1975 we have only 33 more months, or 25 more months or only a few months, to do this work. How many hours did you put in this month? We have only 25 more months; since your money is not going to be worth anything in 25 more months what are you doing with it?"

So I knew people who sold their homes and their businesses, people who put off surgical procedures and sent off all their money to the Watchtower Society during this time. But I had big questions. I heard them saying everything was ending, the world as we knew it would be over in 1975 and we should be working hard door-to-door and sending our money to the Society's headquarters. However, my big questions in 1974 were, "If it's all going down in '75 why are they still building Kingdom Halls? Why was the Watchtower still printing magazines? Why were they still buying new printing presses?" So what they were saying and what they were doing weren't matching up.

By the way, in any relationship, whether it is with an individual or an organization, listen to what they say and watch what they do to see if those two things match up. If they do, great! That's a person or an organization with integrity. However, if they don't, if what they say and what they do does not match up, then beware. There is something definitely wrong. What a person or an organization does is far more telling than what they say. What they are doing is a bigger expression of how they think than what they say.

So, of course, 1975 came and went. I knew one family in particular who had four children. They had calculated how much money they would need to live until October of 1975. They had talked it over with the Circuit Overseer. He assured them that they should sell their home and things they didn't need, move into a rented apartment, keep only what they needed to live until October of '75 and send all the excess to the Society. And of course the autumn of '75 came and went and there they were.

I had a friend who was elderly and living on a pension. It was one in which she could assign the benefits to a different beneficiary in her lifetime. She was coerced to keep enough for her to live on till the autumn of '75 and to give the rest to the Society. So people were told that this was going to happen and they believed it. Then when it didn't happen we were told we were the ones who made the mistake. And, I might add, no one got their money back.

Their truth keeps changing; the truth taught today might change slightly tomorrow. You have to know the 'right answers'. There is a lot of pressure to know the 'right answers' and to always give the 'right answers'.

There is a constant pressure to give time, there are the meetings, there is all the preparation to make sure you have the right answers and there is separation from your friends and your family. You are not to participate in outside activity, but only in what goes on within the congregations.

There is also a concern that if they have not preached to you and you are destroyed at Armageddon then your blood is on their head. So there is a fear of bloodguilt. They believe that Satan and his demons mislead people primarily through false religion. They believe that only 144,000 go to heaven and that the rest of mankind will live on the earth forever.

Separation from Friends and Family

When you become one of Jehovah's Witnesses you are discouraged from associating with family members who are not Witnesses unless it is to try to convert them. So every family function becomes a discussion about the Watchtower, which doesn't make the Witness popular with the family. The Witness cannot attend family dinners on holidays or birthdays or any events that honors a person and holds them in esteem. The leadership of the Watchtower teaches it is usurping God's position to put a person in a place of honor.

The same holds true for friends. You must give up your 'worldly' friends because they will be discouraging to you. The only time you would be with them would be to 'witness' to them in an attempt to convert them to the 'truth'.

I had a very good friend, she and I were full time Pioneers (doorknockers). Someone who goes door-to-door for 100 hours a month and meets certain requirements is called a 'Pioneer'. Back in Philadelphia when we were in our early 20's. Her mother, who was a Witness, was married to a wonderful man who was not a Witness. When this man died quite suddenly her mother was distraught. This was her second husband. Years before this her son had drowned when he was quite young and now her husband had died and she was extremely overwhelmed. She began smoking and was disfellowshipped for it.

Her mother was alone, in her 50's and not well physically. So my friend would go to her mother's home once a week to make dinner and sit and chat with her. My friend was disfellowshipped for associating with her mother because her mother was disfellowshipped for smoking. Can you see the harshness in that? Can you see any love in that? Can you see the fear it sets up? Can you see the spying and reporting that goes on? There is a lot of fear and a lot of things like that happening.

Cultural Isolation

You might wonder how someone could be culturally isolation while still living among other people with different ideas, beliefs and philosophies. If there are enough rules in place to make you different, you are isolated. So what are the rules that accomplish this level of control?

Rules

There are lots of rules that also have to be followed. I made a list of the rules that I could remember and the things I remember my children being subjected to as well. For Jehovah's Witnesses it's important to know what the rules are, because if you break one of them, you will be approached for a discussion about why you broke one of the rules. If you break a rule whether or not you are not sorry or repentant, then you could be disfellowshipped. This is a severe form of ex-communication where someone is put out of the organization. If that happens, everyone must treat you as if you are dead, including your family.

These are some of the things that Jehovah's Witnesses cannot do, say or participate in:

- There are no holidays, none! No holidays are celebrated at all. No Christmas, Thanksgiving, Easter, Halloween, birthdays or any other special days. On holidays the children in school have to go to the office to sit there or you keep them home or they have to sit in the classroom and watch the other children doing the things they cannot do.

- There are no birthdays, no birthday parties. My children did not have birthday parties growing up. I gave my daughter her first birthday party when she was 13 and my son's at 19. That year was also the first time they celebrated Christmas.

- There is no Mother's Day and no Father's Day.

- They don't salute the flag. There was a funny story about this actually. We used to live in southern California and I used to go to Mexico frequently. My daughter usually went with me, but this time it got really interesting. My daughter's father is Italian and so she has an olive complexion. When we came back across the border the American Border Patrol thought I was bringing back a Mexican child. She was about six at the time. So the border guard, wanting to establish that she was American and went to an American school, asked her to say the pledge of allegiance to the flag. She didn't know it. She said, "I don't know it." The guard said "Mom why doesn't she know the pledge of allegiance?" I gave the standard Watchtower answer. "The Constitution says she doesn't have to know it." He then asked her birthday, and because she never had a party to celebrate it there was no huge incentive for a six year old to know it. I then had to explain who we were and answer questions myself before he would let us cross back into the US.

- Cannot sing the national anthem or any patriotic songs.

- Cannot join the military or have any government job as a civilian. Nor can you support the military through donations, meetings, fund-raisers or special days to honor veterans. During the era of the 'draft' Jehovah's Witnesses went to prison as conscientious objectors rather than serve in a non-combatant post as part of the military.

- Cannot say "God bless you" when someone sneezes.

- At the time I was in, you couldn't have pierced ears or tattoos.

- Never wish anyone good luck.

- Don't read books, magazines or novels because you shouldn't really have enough time to do that.

- All friends should be only Jehovah's Witnesses. You don't have friends who aren't Witnesses.

- Limited association with family members who are not Witnesses.

- Cannot date a non-Witness.

- No casual dating. Women never ask men out and men only ask a woman out if he has serious intent toward her. Even then it is recommended that they be chaperoned.

- Cannot sing Christmas carols.

- Above all you don't make a lot of money. Because if you make a lot of money that means you either are, or will become, materialistic. People who come into the organization who are already professionals have one of two experiences. Either they end up having to help a lot of people or they are considered to be materialistic and kept at arms length. They really should give up their dental practice or their medical practice. They should give these things up and live at a lower economic level.

- Don't develop talents.

- Never take art, drama, modeling, or any other classes.

- Don't seek higher education because you won't need it. Armageddon is coming.

- If you are an artist you are not to sign your work and bring glory to yourself.

- No dance classes or any classes for children to develop a talent. I put my daughter in ballet and tap dance classes because I thought that was an important part of growing up. But I had a lot of problems with that and the elders called meetings, asking why was she taking ballet and how could I allow her to take this class and appear in shows locally.

- Don't ask questions of the leadership.

- Cannot have blood transfusions or donate blood.

- This next one looks funny until I explain it, but you don't buy a two-door car. You see a two-door car makes it hard for people going door-to-door to get in and out of the back seat. A station wagon, an estate car or a van is the best form of transportation.

- Cannot go to psychiatrists, psychologists or counselors.

- Cannot see marriage counselors. Instead of professional help you will be offered a Bible study with one of the elders in the congregation. If you have marital problems up to and including infidelity, mental or physical abuse, you will be disfellowshipped for gossiping if you discuss it with anyone whether a professional or a friend.

- If you come into the Watchtower and you have a history of drug abuse you cannot take methadone nor can you attend AA. At least you couldn't when I was involved with them. They have a procedure where you are disfellowshipped if you do something they consider to be 'unchristian'. So if you are an alcoholic and you have a problem with alcoholism you will be disfellowshipped but you will not be permitted to go to AA and if you do they will not allow you to come back into the organization. If you have not been disfellowshipped and you are in the organization and you go to AA you will be disfellowshipped.

Disfellowshipping could be for a term of one or two years and then the person could apply for reinstatement. During that term of one or two years if the person wants to be reinstated he or she would have to attend the meetings even though no one could talk to them and there could be no conversations or activities in or out of the meeting hall with any of Jehovah's Witnesses.

- There is no sports participation. My son is over six feet tall and looks like a major league football player. All through high school teachers and coaches were asking him to be on the football team. More than one coach told him he could get a football scholarship. My son is a big guy and would have been really good, but we couldn't allow him to participate in sports because of belonging to the Watchtower organization. The high school games were on Saturdays and he had to go door-to-door. There were no exceptions.

- There is no after school recreation.

- No school politics.

- No little league.

- No bowling team.

- The kids can't go to the YMCA for any reason.

- No smoking.

- Cannot miss meetings for any reason.

- Cannot work over time or accept promotions if it will interfere with you attending all the meetings and going door-to-door.

- Cannot vote.

- If you work in a shop you can't sell cigarettes.

- Cannot belong to any social clubs, groups, bowling leagues, craft groups or any other group that socializes with non-Witnesses.

- Cannot attend social functions sponsored by their employer including Christmas parties, summer barbecues or awards dinners unless it is made mandatory for employment.

- Cannot socialize with co-workers after hours.

- At work it was recommended that your lunch hour be spent alone with your lunch and your Bible and not socializing with other people.

- Cannot disagree with the organizations rules of conduct or their doctrines.

- Cannot campaign for any political candidate, discuss politics or hold public office.

- Cannot be a union steward or shop steward nor be involved in a union strike.

- Cannot become a police officer if a gun is required.

- No Yoga classes.

- No alternate medical assistance such as Rheiki, Reflexology, Aromatherapy, Indian head massage, or other holistic healing methods.

- No meditation or quieting the mind. It is thought that to quiet the mind is to allow demonic thoughts to enter.

- Do not refer to yourself as a human 'being', but as a human. They say only God is a being and we cannot claim that description.

- Cannot read books, magazines or pamphlets from other religions or belief systems.

- Cannot buy anything from a church garage sale or donate anything to a church run store.

- Cannot donate money to any charities for any cause.

- Cannot shop at or work for the Salvation Army or Goodwill or any other charity shop.

- Cannot go to the prom or school dances.

- Cannot attend class reunions.

- Never be hypnotized.

- Cannot joint Boy Scouts, Girl Scouts, Brownies, Girl Guides or other youth groups.

- Cannot serve on Jury Duty.

- Never study psychology, philosophy, sociology or cultural viewpoints because those studies might shake their faith.

- Never attend other Christian churches, nondenominational churches, mosques, synagogues or any other non-Witness place of learning or worship.

- Cannot get married in another church.

- No sex or sexual contact before marriage.

- Certain sexual practices are prohibited after marriage between married people.

- Breaking an engagement can result in disciplinary action.

- Cannot be gay or lesbian.

- Cannot throw rice at a wedding.

- Never make or participate in a toast with a drink.

- No raffle tickets, bingo or gambling of any sort.

- Cannot sing any holiday songs or any patriotic songs.

- No blue jeans, shorts or casual clothing at the Kingdom Hall or home study groups.

- Women are not to wear slacks to the Kingdom Hall.

- Women are not to wear slacks or colored tights going door-to-door no matter how cold the weather.

- Women cannot hold positions of responsibility in the congregation, speak from the platform or pray in the congregation.

- Men cannot have long hair or facial hair.

- Never say anything negative about the organization.

- Never do or say anything that would reflect negatively on the organization even if it means covering over wrongdoing.

- Never take another Jehovah's Witness to court.

- Cannot own or wear a cross or have a cross in your home.

- Cannot own any religious pictures or statues of any kind.

- Cannot look into or discuss witchcraft, black or white magic or consult with a psychic.

- Cannot participate in any psychic activity even if you have psychic abilities.

- There is NO involvement at all with tarot cards, numerology, astrology, ESP, mediums, superstitions or prophesying.

- No speaking in tongues or laying on of hands.

- No combat training, boxing, wrestling or martial arts of any kind.

- Women cannot be elders or hold any position of responsibility in the congregation.

- Cannot greet, speak or socialize with someone who has been disfellowshipped or who has disassociated themselves.

- Must not keep secrets from the organization. If you know someone is doing something considered 'unchristian' you must report it.

- When you have a problem of any kind, whether you are an adult or a child, there is no support or help for you. Children will be disfellowshipped for stealing, lying or other things that children do when they are showing signs of needing help of some kind. There is no love shown to anyone in trouble or with a problem but there is judgment and punishment that results in mental torment and emotional abuse.

The list goes on and on, but you can see how restrictive life becomes. When life is this restrictive you are isolated from the community around you including your neighbors, former friends, school friends, work mates and everyone whom you meet.

We / They Thinking

It's easy to see how so many rules would keep you isolated and separated from other people. Of course, they are taught that this is for their protection and these rules keep them in line with Jehovah's desire for them to follow Him wholeheartedly. They are told these rules will protect them from people who would interfere with their faith. Jehovah's Witnesses believe that everyone outside of the Watchtower organization has evil intent. They believe that outsiders are not honest or faithful in their marriages and that they have no innate moral integrity.

Jehovah's Witnesses expect persecution because it confirms to them that they have 'The Truth'. They have been inculcated with the belief that it is "us against the world".

Recreation is limited to those things going on within the congregation. There is a real 'we/they' mentality. This is another mark of a cult. It's another mark of any controlling relationship. It's us against them. We have the truth they don't. We will survive they won't. So when a Witness is at your door that is the framework that they are coming from. It's not a conversation in mutuality. It's coming from a mental framework that says, "I've got the truth and I'm going to survive. You're not going to survive, and you can only survive if you listen to me. You can make it through Armageddon if you listen to me and are willing to hold a Bible study with me." So because of that kind of thinking you're really set up to be separate.

Your vocabulary is also dictated and controlled. As an example, Witnesses don't say 'bulletin board'. They say 'information board'. Do you know why? Because the word 'bulletin' comes from the Latin for the papal bulls that used to be nailed to the doors of the churches -- that's where the word 'bulletin' comes from. So in keeping separate they use the phrase 'information board'.

I'm trying to think of some of the other words they use that are different. It's been a long time. But that's one that stands out. They don't have 'potluck' dinners they have 'covered dish' dinners. Things don't happen by 'chance' but because 'time and unforeseen occurrence befalls them all'. There are a lot of other little things. Their vocabulary is different and it sets them apart. The more that you are involved with them, the more everything you do and say is controlled.

Uniformity of Beliefs

We've discussed many of the beliefs they hold and you've heard the endless rules that must be obeyed or there will be consequences of some sort. What is amazing for most people to hear though is all Jehovah's Witnesses must believe exactly the same thing. They are not permitted to question anything. And they are very used to being careful to always say the right thing and to have the right answers.

Sometimes you may have somebody come to your church who has left this organization or any other cult or legalistic church (churches with excessive rules) and you wonder why, when you have tried to be friendly, they never come back. Or perhaps, you have befriended, or would like to get to know someone better, who has come out of a controlling relationship of some kind. You've been kind, you've extended yourself and yet, you don't get the response you were expecting.

Keep in mind, you are talking to someone who has had to have the 'right answers' or be humiliated, has been culturally isolated and may not know the current events and trends that you do, has had someone else making all of their decisions for them, and who has lost their sense of identity, authority and autonomy. And so, innocently we may say something that will trigger the same guilt they have experienced in their previous relationship or involvement with one of these kinds of organizations.

As an example, they may come to church one Sunday and then miss the next Sunday and when you see them you say, "Oh I missed you last week are you okay?" You mean it as showing interest, but that question will put the person back into the heavy guilt that you never miss meetings, even if you're sick and no matter how old you're children are. My daughter was born on a Wednesday and on Sunday we were at the Kingdom Hall with my six-year-old son. And the following Saturday we were door-to-door. You just cannot let up. When my son was born we were going door-to-door in the snow on the Upper Peninsula of Michigan in January when he was just two weeks old.

Loss of Individualism
I think you can see how, over time with this complete control and isolation you begin to

lose sight of who you are. You start out being captivated by what you hear and you end up being a captive to their control. You are kept so busy you don't notice what's happening until it's too late. Your own hopes and dreams get forgotten. Your talents and skills are discounted, not encouraged and left by the wayside because of lack of time and the control. Anything you worked hard to achieve prior to coming into the Watchtower has been discredited and discarded. You spend your day thinking, speaking, planning, studying, preparing or doing whatever it is that will further the work of the Watchtower Bible and Tract Society.

There is a lack of personal authority. You do not make too many decisions on your own. Everything is decided for you so it's very difficult when you come out of a cult, or any relationship in which you have been controlled, to have any sense of personal authority. It's difficult to realize that you can make choices or that you can decide what you want for your future. Life is lived on hold in this organization. You're always waiting for Armageddon and never planning for your own personal dreams or goals.

As I said earlier, this is especially true if you are a woman. In the Watchtower, men make all the decisions. It's a very male dominated organization. There has to be conformity of thought. Everybody believes exactly the same thought about every subject all around the world. I knew Witnesses in Mexico, in Canada and we had people who would come to visit us from around the world. Everyone thought alike, or at least said the 'right things'. Everybody believes the same thing on every topic. Ask a question and you'll get the same answer. There's no room for personal thoughts or opinions

Stage 6 – Detailed Accountability / Spying / Lack of Personal Authority / Lack of Joy / Life on 'Hold'

Detailed Accountability

When we went door-to-door we would have to fill in a report form every week. When we were Special Pioneering we would have to send them directly to the Watchtower Society's headquarters in Brooklyn, New York. But when you're part of the congregation you turn them in by putting them in a box at the back of the Kingdom Hall. This is called a Publisher's Weekly Field Report. Everybody who is an active participant in the congregation is called a publisher because you publish good tidings, good news.

Down the side of this report are all the days of the week and across the top it has columns for you to report books that you have placed at the door as well as booklets, subscriptions, back calls, Bible studies and magazines.

You report the hours spent in preaching activity each day. New subscriptions are reported. If you talk to someone at the door and you signed him or her up for a six month or one year subscription to The Watchtower or Awake magazines you put that down as well as individual magazine. You would report back calls. A back call is when you have had a discussion with someone at the door and you go back again to see that person. When you go to the same house two or three times and have discussions you would begin to call that a Bible study and that's put down too. Each column is totaled for the week.

You can see there is little or no time for any activities outside of the Watchtower requirements and your home and family so you do become isolated and separated from your friends and extended family by the unreasonable demands on your time and energy.

These reports get turned in every week. Then the reports get transferred to what is called a Publisher's Record Card. This is a card that reports your weekly activity for a longer period of time, usually a year. If you don't turn in one of these weekly reports for three months then your publisher's record card gets moved to the back of the box they are kept in.

When the Circuit Overseer, who oversees the 20 or so congregations in a circuit, remember we talked about that earlier, when he visits the congregation, these are the people he's concerned about and wants to know what's going on. What's happened? Who's working with these people? What's the problem?

He is concerned because the Watchtower teaches that these people might not survive Armageddon when it comes because their cards are in the back of the box. That may sound bizarre to you, but these are some the things that keep a Witness working. There is a concern that they could be destroyed for eternity.

Spying

I attended a Passover celebration at the invitation of a Jewish friend just a few months before I left the Watchtower. Another Witness worked as a waitress for the caterer who was catering the event. That Witness called the elders and told them I had attended this gathering so the elders called a meeting with me because of my attending this Jewish celebration. The meeting they called for me to attend to address my 'sinful behavior' is called a 'Committee Meeting' and was intended to intimidate and frighten me and to condemn any activity that is considered 'un-Christian'.

I told them I would not be attending such a meeting and that we could discuss it here and now on the phone or not at all. The elder on the phone wasn't sure what to do with that because that response was completely unexpected. So he agreed to discuss it on the phone. After he told me the 'charge' against me I said, "Help me understand. I attended this Passover Celebration and I'm being brought before you on charges of unchristian conduct, while she served all these people, thereby helping them to celebrate the Passover, and she is not guilty of any wrong doing. What's wrong with this picture?" The elder on the phone did not like the question. Who they decide to pursue is very selective.   The elder on the phone was so completely caught off guard that nothing further was done.

A witness would say that spying never happens, but in reality it does. Just like this phone call to the elders from the caterer's assistant about my attending the Passover.

After 21 years of marriage my husband wanted to separate. The interesting thing was, I found that I was the one being very closely monitored. At the time there was nothing going on in my life worth monitoring. I would come home from work and find someone parked across from my house to make sure I was coming straight home from work. I would get phone calls at 1:00 and 2:00 in the morning, waking me and checking on me. Yet before this, I would have said that there was no spying – no checking up on people. I would have been the first one to tell you before my experience that things like that never happen. But I experienced it first hand and I'm here to tell you that spying does go on.

Lack of Personal Authority

In any controlling relationship, and especially in the Watchtower, you cannot make decisions for yourself about where you want to go or whom you want to associate with. When you become part of them you give up your choices to be curious, lead a normal life or do anything outside of the organization.

As an example, if you are a woman, you are under the control of your husband. Husbands are the undisputed heads of their households. A wife cannot pray in the presence of her husband because he is her head and he is to represent the family and his wife in prayer. A wife can pray with her children unless she has a son who has been baptized as one of Jehovah's Witnesses. Then he must be the one who prays if they are together.

There was an article that came out in the 70's that said that a sister (men and women in the congregation are called 'brother' and 'sister') was not to disagree with a brother speaking from the platform "even by the expression on her face".

Lack of Joy

So you are separated from family and friends and eventually you experience cultural isolation. Believe it or not, I have heard that the CIA actually studied what goes on in that organization because they don't understand how you can culturally isolate someone without removing them from society. And it is a total cultural isolation. There is no participation in anything that goes on outside of it. Everything you expose yourself to is selected by the organization.

Life is just about work and becomes so tedious and tiresome that you lose your joy. You lose the sense that life is wonderful and happy with unlimited possibilities. Life in the Watchtower is about work, doing the right thing, thinking the right thing and saying the right thing. There is very little joy in an individual's life or family, but they get very good at smiling in the group.

Life on 'Hold'

Let's talk about your occupation. I don't know what the situation is now, but I left in 1984 and up until that time most people were encouraged to not go beyond high school. And, in fact, they were encouraged not in writing and not in print, but there was verbal encouragement, that once you reached the legal age to terminate your education, which in most states was 14, you should then go door-to-door full time. So there is a high preponderance of people who have no education beyond the age of 14. As time went by and Armageddon didn't come as predicted, these young people grew to be adults who found difficulty getting jobs without even a high school diploma. There was no encouragement for anyone to get an education or a higher paid job or to further himself or herself in any way. In fact, higher education as actively discouraged.

People were discouraged from planning for their retirement because the end was always just around the corner. People would reach their 50's and 60's with no savings and no pension. They would have spent their entire lives going door-to-door and conducting these studies and attending meetings and had nothing to fall back on when they were too old to work.

When I first came into the organization in 1960 I can remember people who kept their children from starting school for as long as possible because they believed Armageddon was coming any day and their children didn't need school. So children were starting school as late as 7 or 8 when the authorities stepped in.

In addition, when I first came into that organization, they were still discouraging people from having children. The teaching was that the end was near and why would you want to bring children into this old system of things and take your time away from going door-to-door and placing magazines and books. Back then, in the 60's when someone got pregnant people weren't happy for you. Babies were a serious interruption to 'the work'. So many people came to their retirement age with no family and no savings.

Stage 7 – Trapped / No One to Turn To / Weariness / Fear of Losing Family, Friends and Eternity

Trapped / No One to Turn To

You are kept constantly busy with no time to think. You see, with the meeting preparation you don't have time for reading novels and magazines even if it was approved. Then you have to study for Tuesday night and study for the two hours for Thursday night. In addition, you've got to study for the hour long Watchtower Study on Sunday because you are expected to raise your hand whether or not you are called on. You've also got to study for your family Bible study and at least one other Bible study you are going to have with another family within the community. So all that keeps you very, very busy.

Before you can place any books at the door you have to have read them. And you also have to read the entire Watchtower and all the Awake magazines before you take them door-to-door and there's two of each every month. There are two Watchtower magazines and two Awake magazines each and every month. So there's no time to do anything else. You're trapped and there's no one to turn to. There's no one you can share those kinds of feelings with.

Weariness
I want to share with you that the people who come to your door are real people. They are people who hurt, they are people who struggle, and they are people with children. They are people with a tremendous burden, with a horrendous schedule, with a tremendous amount of guilt, with a lot of drive, with a lot of pressure and they are tired. A lot of them are tired. A lot of them are weary. I went door-to-

door for 24 years. 150 hours per month for several of those years and 100 hours a month for a few more of those years. I usually went 20 to 30 hours a month for the majority of the time.

Fear of Losing Family and Friends

So many times a Witness will be afraid to leave because members of their family are Witnesses. Perhaps it is their spouse, children or their parents. They know that if they leave their family members will no longer treat them the same. They will speak to them only when they have to. The phone calls will stop from relatives not living in the same home. Their husband or wife will not be able to treat them in the same way and a distance will grow in the marriage. The believing mate will be sympathized with and will continue to take the children to the meetings and door-to-door so the rift grows wider between the parent who left and their child. It is a very distressing thing to see when one family member leaves.

The fear of losing friends is strong. When I left the Watchtower, people who I had known for 24 years cut off the relationship. Formerly close friends who saw me on the street would cross to the other side rather than have to acknowledge me. I remember at my daughter's graduation I sat behind a Witness couple I knew. She turned to look at me, turned very red and whispered to her husband and they never turned to me directly. When it was over you would have thought they were shot out of a cannon they left so quickly.

I think you get the picture of how what I call 'The Wedge of Involvement' works. We've talked about the seven stages and how it starts out so well and ends up so painful. However, while I was part of this organization there were many interesting experiences and many things I learned that have been extremely helpful to me in my life. No situation is all bad, just as none are all good. There is a mix of both in everything that we participate in.

My life today is very happy and extremely fulfilling. My regrets center around my children and what they were deprived of growing up. While I cannot give them back their childhood I remember a sign I once saw that said, "It's never too late to have a happy childhood." None of us have had a perfect childhood. Or at least very few have. So as adults we have all had to make our way through our individual challenges and learn to enjoy our lives both 'in spite of' and 'because of' our past. I can only trust that my children, who are now grown, can believe that is true.

My husband was a Congregation Overseer when we were in Michigan, where my son was born, but we had to leave the Upper Peninsula of Michigan because of health reasons. We moved to Tucson, where again my husband held a position in the congregation. We were there for seven years and during that time I gave birth to my daughter. I thought I had the perfect family. We then moved to California. After a few years in California we were asked to work in a Spanish area. I don't speak Spanish but learnt enough to witness at the door and speak some simple Spanish. I could conduct a very basic Bible study but my Spanish was just enough to get me into trouble and not good enough to get me out of it.

I once prayed in Spanish and asked God to forgive us for our fish. So that ended my praying in Spanish. I found this door-to-door record in Spanish from when we were working in that territory. (Holding up the Spanish record form for recording field activity). We had some very interesting experiences.

My first marriage ended in 1983. The following summer I was sitting in a stadium in San Diego at one of the large assemblies held by Jehovah's Witnesses. This was the first assembly where I had not interpreted for the deaf. Usually I would be in front of the section reserved for the deaf and hard of hearing and I would be just so busy interpreting that I was not really taking it in. It's like everything is just passing through my ears to my hands. This was the first time I actually just sat and listened. I was sitting there with my daughter who was 12 at that time, and I looked out over the crowd and thought, "For 24 years this has been my family. I don't really know anybody outside the Watchtower. This is my family. This is my home. This is the rest of my life." And as clearly as I am standing before you I heard a voice inside my head say to me, "These aren't your people, this isn't your family. Get up and leave and don't ever come back."

I mean have you ever had a voice in your head speak to you that clearly? I turned to my daughter and I said, "Let's leave," and she said, "Ok." So we left and went out into the parking lot and I thought, "Well, now where do we go?"

When someone leaves The Watchtower there is a lot of fear. There is no one to turn to. There is no one to ask anything of. You certainly can't ask anything of another Witness. They will think you're crazy and that Satan has hold of your mind. I did not know anyone who was safe to talk to. I knew if I left the Watchtower I'd lose my friends, I'd lose everybody I'd known and been close to for the past 24 years.

I was standing in the parking lot and thinking, "Ok, I left and now where do I go?" Then I remembered that about a month earlier there had been an article in the newspaper where some ex-Witnesses had been interviewed. I went down to the newspaper office to look up that article and I got their names. I called directory enquiries and they were listed. A really nice lady answered the phone with a Canadian accent and it turned out her name was Marjorie. We chatted for about an hour and she said, "You've got to come on over tonight." She gave me her address and said, "I know you'll find my door." And I did! Witnesses will find any door anywhere in the world. We were fearless. We did not know the meaning of rejection. That was not in our vocabulary.

When I got to her door a man answered the doorbell and looked at me. It was someone I had known 20 years earlier when we were in Escanaba, Michigan. He was a fourth generation Witness. He was on the Upper Peninsula of Michigan when were there and I knew he had left the Watchtower, but, I thought he was in Canada yet here he was standing at a door in southern California. I looked at him and I hadn't seen him in nearly 21 years. I said, "Jim what are you doing here?" All he did was open the door and he said, "Welcome to freedom."

When I went in I learned that he and his wife were on a sabbatical for one year and this was their first day of that sabbatical. They had come to stay with Marjorie and her husband, Leonard, while they looked for an apartment. When he heard who was on the phone he said to Marjorie, "I've got to answer this door." He said that he would never have believed that I would have walked out of the Watchtower. But that year over 100,000 Witnesses walked out. There was a mass exodus.

So he, his wife and I met together weekly along with their daughter for the balance of that year. And they helped me to turn around some of the thinking I had adopted while in that organization.

I've gone door-to-door in Michigan, Illinois, Arizona, California, and even in Denver. If you lived anywhere near Englewood, you probably met me 20 years ago. Believe it or not, with the thousands of doors I knocked on over the years, I can probably count on one hand the number of people who knew their Bible and who were kind. I met a lot of people who knew their Bible but they were not necessarily kind.

When I came out, besides my new friends that I made as a result of that phone call, I thought, "Well, who do I know who can I just sit down with and talk to?" There had been a Baptist pastor in the territory that I had been assigned to who had literally one day at his door grabbed my Bible out of my hand and angrily threw it at me while yelling at me to leave his property. Now, he may have been able to help me but there was no way I was going back to that person.

There was a woman whom I did know whose husband was a Baptist pastor and so I went to him and he told me he got a whole new degree after talking to me for several months.

He said he thought he'd learned a lot about the Bible in college. But his meetings together with me to answer my questions and refute the Watchtower doctrine meant he was really digging and looking for some answers.

In the course of this series we are going to be showing you a film that Marjorie and Leonard, whom I talked to that first day, have made. It is a first rate video on Jehovah's Witnesses. They have also written a book called, "Witnesses of Jehovah". They are wonderful people and I highly recommend their book and their video, which are both available through Amazon.com or Amazon.co.uk.

But what can you say if one of Jehovah's Witnesses comes to your door? Yes it's tempting to say you're busy. But, rather than saying you're busy and shutting the door which is a natural inclination, let them know that if they ever have any questions and would like to talk about the Bible without a Watchtower, yours is a safe home to come to. That this is a safe place to come back to and ask questions. At least tell them that so that they know when they feel that urge in their heart to do something they have somewhere to go. I can guarantee that they will have your address written down. They will be able to come back and speak with you. I met many people who knew the Bible but no one who was safe to go back to. So let them know that you can be that safe place for them.

If you don't know your Bible well enough to feel comfortable offering to answer questions, then offer to be a friend. Just having a listening ear that has no judgment is a huge thing when someone leaves this or any other controlling environment.

The whole purpose in talking about cults and talking about false teaching is not to expose a people, because these people have good hearts. But it is to expose those teachings that are taking advantage of those good hearts.

I knew six people in the Watchtower who committed suicide because of the pressures. Three of them were teenagers. You will see the parents of one of those people in this video. Their son was an 18 when he killed himself and you'll hear his story. These are a people who have been under a tremendous fear and pressure.

As you see the video you will have a lot of questions that come up and you may have had a lot of questions from last week. I'm going to sit down in about 20 seconds or less because this video is 58 minutes long and I want you to see the whole thing and then we can take 15 or 20 minutes afterward for questions if you are able to stay. If you can't we can address some of them tomorrow night.

(The video was shown at this point. If you want to see this you can order it from Amazon.com or Amazon.co.uk.)

Questions and Answers after watching the video: (The questions are directly quoted from audience participants)

1. After watching the video how does a Witness know if they should take communion or not?

Answer: The majority of Witnesses are told they are going to live on the earth and their eternal life is because they are associating with the 144,000. Only those who believe that they are amongst the 144,0000 who are left on the earth actually partake of communion. I think today there are between 6,000 to 7,000 who claim to be part of that group. Most of the Witnesses who claim this hope are elderly.

Jehovah's Witnesses have a meeting once a year called 'The Memorial'. It's held on a date in the Hebrew calendar, which is Nisan 14, or commonly known as Passover. They count the number of people who partake of the bread and the wine and that number is sent to the Watchtower headquarters from around the world. That is how they come up with a number for the balance of the 144,000 who are left.

2. Question: In the video, Jesus is portrayed as Michael the Archangel. He showed what they believe is the end of the world and he is throwing all these fireballs. It looks like in the cartoon there that everyone was dying. Back in the Old Testament when Noah built the ark only a selective few were saved. How are the selective few of the JW's saved? It looks like everybody was getting flooded out or burned up or whatever?

Answer: I'll give you the answer to that and then I'll tell you a funny story. The answer is they believe God will find a way to protect each of them in the midst of that holocaust.

They believe they will somehow be identified and protected by Him. There will be a select few who will survive Armageddon. The only ones who survive will be baptized Witnesses who are going door-to-door.

Back in 1957 or '58 in Philadelphia, there was a tremendous storm. It was a very unusual storm. There were hailstones the size of golf balls and bigger coming down. Nobody had ever seen weather like this before. It happened to be on a night there was a meeting in the Kingdom Hall. So everyone who was inside the hall thought Armageddon was starting. All the people in the neighborhood had been hearing about 'the end' coming because of the Witnesses going door-to-door so they started pouring into the Kingdom hall thinking that it was Armageddon. When the storm ended they went home and didn't come back.

3. Question: What do you say to these people when they do come knocking at your door? I would imagine that they are closed, just like other cults. They don't let you talk. Do we have to actually just be rude and say no thank you and shut the door?

Answer: That is a great question because we think we need to be able to argue with them or be able to refute them but it doesn't work. Of all the people I know who've come out of the Watchtower none of them have come out because they were argued with. You might win the argument but you will lose the war.

The biggest thing, and I can't say this strongly enough, is to let them know your home is a safe place to come back too. That if they ever want to ask a question and not refer to the Watchtower magazines or books, but use only the Bible, your home is a safe place to come to. Or if they feel the need to just have a safe place to come to talk, your home is that safe place.

4. Question: Does that mean you should study with them?

Answer: Never study with them. I know so many people, and I'm one of them, who studied with them to prove them wrong. I know of pastors who did that and then became Witnesses. So you never want to get involved in a prolonged conversation on a repeated basis. Just let them know this is a safe home that you will pick the subject and help them understand the Bible and the message of love. But let them know you are not interested in the prepared sermon they have.

5. Question: I know a couple that – his wife is studying – and he has asked me about JW's but she's studying with them and I don't really know them that well. But, how could I approach that as far as them because she's been trying to explain what she's been taught and they just laugh and say you've been lied to all your life and it's a delicate situation. So how would I be able to say here, this is what it is? Because I would think that she would just be in such a state of confusion about what she believes, so what do I do?

Answer: It is a delicate situation and it is very confusing. There are many, many women in the Watchtower with their children and the husband is not involved. It literally divides families. The husband becomes an outsider in his own home. It's a very difficult situation for a family. The best thing you can do is to suggest giving equal time to sit down and just read through the Bible without any outside books.

Walt (my second husband) and I knew a couple when we lived in California, he had been raised in the Watchtower and his fiancé was a young woman in the church we were attending. He was in the military, which meant he had moved away from the Watchtower teaching but those teachings were still in his mind. They had fallen in love and wanted to be married, but before they were married, she wanted him 'deprogrammed', and he really wanted that too. He had a lot of questions and was very confused.

They asked if they could come to our home once a week for a Bible study. I said we could do that on one condition. There would be no books other than the Bible. I'm not going to bring any books and you can't bring any either. All we will have is the Bible. It was important for him to learn he could think for himself and make his own determinations on what he read. They agreed to that. When we studied I would have him read a couple of verses from the book of John and would then ask him what he thought it meant. What is it telling you? What is that saying? He would say the Watchtower said 'so and so', and I would say, "Yes, I know what the Watchtower says, but what does the Bible say? What is it saying here?" So there was no personal interpretation, no leading questions. Simply, "What does it say?"

6. Question: In a meeting like that would they bring their Bible as well?

Answer: They could bring their Bible. In fact, encourage them to bring it and the Greek interlinear. There is a purple Bible they showed in the video. It's called A Greek Interlinear Translation. It's based on Benjamin Wilson's printing plates from the 1800's of the Greek Diaglot. He was not a Witness. He had painstakingly translated the original Greek into English, word for word. The Watchtower bought those plates. I think it was in 1890 or somewhere around then. They then later published their own version, but still used his plates. As you read that, it will show the Greek word and have the exact English word underneath. Over in the margin it will have the translation paraphrased.

When you read what is paraphrased it will read differently from what you read word for word. As an example, wherever the text uses the Greek word Kyrios, which is the Greek word for Lord, they will take the liberty of interpreting that as Jehovah, as God, as Lord, or as Jesus depending on the context and what subtle message they want it to convey. But when you look at the Greek interlinear, where you see the word for word translation, you can see where they have taken liberties in their own translation. If they want to bring their own Bible, ask them to also bring the Greek Interlinear and sit down with both. Let them see the liberties taken in the translation.

7. Question: Do they pray out loud? And do people take turns praying like we pray?

Answer: Yes. They pray out loud, but not spontaneously or taking turns. Prayers are by men only or if no man is present, a woman can pray if her head is covered.

8. Question: We have a neighbor who's a Jehovah's Witness and he's been friendly with my son and yesterday he and my son

took off for the whole day. He's been preaching to my son, but my son still went to youth group that night. What can we do tonight to help my son?

Answer: Keep talking to your son. Find out what he's thinking. You may want to find a way to limit the association or not. Request equal time and invite the neighbor to the youth group.

When one person in a family becomes a JW it can be devastating to a family. It is not an organization of love, but of rules. Your son needs your protection so keep talking and keep the lines of communication open. Find out what he is thinking.

To let you know how seriously the rules are obeyed and the consequences, let me share a personal story. My closest friend was severely injured in an automobile accident and would have lived had she been able to have a blood transfusion. But because the Watchtower forbids blood transfusions, she bled to death internally. I was close to the family and there were three children left with no mother as a result of that crazy rule.

Another family in a congregation we were part of had a child who was born with a heart problem that was correctable with surgery. When the child was 3 years old she died because the parents would not allow a blood transfusion and so would not allow the doctors to go ahead with the operation.

The pressure is so strong. There is so much fear. Life is disposable. The attitude is, "Well if a child does die as a result of taking a stand to support Watchtower teaching, they will come back after Armageddon and, anyway, you can have more children".

You want to protect your son from this kind of thinking; where everything is disposable. It's like living your life on hold and watching a movie. When I came out of the Watchtower it took me a couple of years to really wake up and then I thought where did the last 24 years go? Really, I still wonder where all that time went. I look at that period of my life and think 'that was 24 years'. That's a long time. But yet it was like a blink of an eye because it was as if I had been in a state of sleepwalking.

9. Question: What do Jehovah's Witnesses believe about resurrection?

Answer: They believe the majority of people will be resurrected to the earth and that only 144,000 will be resurrected to the heavens. They also believe that you will only be resurrected if you are one of Jehovah's Witnesses and in Jehovah's favor. Then you may be resurrected after Armageddon. But if you are not in His favor you will not be resurrected. If you are disfellowshipped or have disassociated yourself you will not be resurrected. Disfellowshipping, as I said earlier, is when they take action against you for what they call a wrongdoing. Disassociation is when you take action against them and formally leave.

I wrote a letter of disassociation so they believe that when I die I am dead forever. There is no resurrection for me, or life after death in any form in their thinking. The fear people have in the Watchtower is that by leaving it they will lose their eternal life. They will lose their hope of a resurrection.

10. Question: If they believe that Jehovah provides everything how do they reconcile that Jesus said no one approaches the Father except through Me?

Answer: They believe you do pray in the name of Jesus and that is how you approach Jehovah. But, Jehovah is the one you pray to and He is the one who provides all.

** End of Questions and Answers **

What is it that would prompt someone who has been in the Watchtower that long to leave? I can assure you it is not an argument at the door. An argument at the door does not encourage someone to leave that organization. That just confirms to them that they have the truth and they are being persecuted at your door.

What prompts them to leave? Sometimes it's a life trauma and some reality sets in. They get to see their life has been lived on hold. It may be the death of somebody close to them, it may be a divorce, it may be a close friend or relative being disfellowshipped for seemingly inconsequential reasons or it may be the recognition that none of their prophecies have happened as they said they would. It's during the traumas in life a Witness gets to see that to the leaders in the Watchtower, obeying the rules of the organization is stronger and more important than showing love.

I used to have good friends who lived in Southern California. Their daughter got an apartment of her own. The first terrible thing they thought she did was to get a roommate who was not a Witness. But when that roommate, who was not a Witness, put a pumpkin in her window at Halloween the Witness, my friend's daughter, was disfellowshipped. Even though it was her roommate who performed the act, she was disfellowshipped for un-Christian behavior by allowing the celebration of Halloween in her home. When this happened it meant she was treated as though she was dead and she couldn't even speak with her parents. Things like that will expose the kind of restricted and conditional love that exists. Sometimes it's an exposure of the true motivation behind the organization.

You don't know what is going on in the mind of the Witness who is at your door. You don't really know where they are spiritually or emotionally; usually a stronger one will be with a weaker one. If you can appeal to the heart, the weaker one will come back. If you appeal to the head the stronger one will come back with another stronger one.

I'm going to say this and I'm probably going to say it more than once. Never study with a Witness. You may think you're going to bring them along. You may think you are going to expose what they believe. Trust me! Never study with a Witness because it doesn't usually end up the way you think it will. They are very persuasive. You may not want to say anything more at the door than what we shared earlier. Which is, "If you ever want to come back without the Watchtower and just really ask some questions or just talk, this is a safe place to come and I really wish you well. Have a great day!"

Hopefully, this has given you some idea of what is going on in the life and in the mind of the person who is ringing your doorbell. If they ever decide to leave, they will need a safe place to come to. If you meet someone like this, who has come out of this very painful involvement, or if you have a neighbor or relative who leaves a controlling relationship of any kind, you could be that safe person for them so long as you keep a few things in mind:

1. Encourage them to find their own path, their own way. Don't try to force them to join you on your path.

2. Appreciate their individuality – compliment them on those things you see that are unique to them.

3. Answer their questions honestly and openly. If you don't know the answer, tell them you don't and help them find it.

4. Listen to them when they are ready to talk about things, but don't push them into talking before they are ready.

5. Don't judge them with questions such as "How could you be part of such a thing?" or statements like, "You seem too smart to have been involved!"

6. Invite them to fun things such as going out to lunch or a movie where they can relax.

7. Introduce them to your friends and help them to widen their circle and meet people who are trustworthy and safe.

In Conclusion...

One of the things that helped me the most when I left the Watchtower was to look at the things I learned while I was one of Jehovah's Witnesses that had benefitted me. In our life there are things we perceive as good and benefiting us and there are things we perceive as negative, or challenging us. Usually we stand on one end of this spectrum or another and refuse to see the other side. This is a very unbalanced view and makes life difficult in so many ways.

When we can see an equal amount of benefits to challenges, we move into a much more balanced perspective, a more balanced view of life and it relieves the stress, reduces the fear, dissolves the anger and allows us to grow as a result of our experience.

The things I saw to be beneficial for me were those things that were unique for me. You will see things that will make sense to you and will help you to heal from the emotional and spiritual wounds much more quickly.

Whether you are someone who has left a very legalistic and controlling group or relationship, or whether you want to be available as a safe person for others who will need that refuge, I am so very glad that you've been here to listen for these four nights. I pray that you will continue to extend love to yourself and others and that you will appreciate the wonderful, magnificent creation you are as you receive from and contribute into this amazing experience of life.

Thank you.

A message from the author…

The effect on both men and women from an extended period of time in a controlling group or relationship is traumatic. When children are raised in such an environment they may blame their parents for the results they are dealing with as adults and when adults enter such a relationship by choice they may blame themselves or wonder how they could have let that happen.

It doesn't matter how you got involved. The important thing is that you got out. If you are still in the relationship, then congratulate yourself on being brave enough to have read this book to this point and know that there is help and there is light at the end of the tunnel for you. You can create the kind of life you want to enjoy now that you see you have the right to make your own choices and no one can take control of you again unless you let them.

When I first left the Watchtower I met with a group of women with teen-aged daughters once a month for about a year. Those twelve meetings proved invaluable. We discovered our daughters all had several symptoms in common as a result of being raised in such a male dominated society that only occasionally gave lip service to honoring women. Their actions and words didn't match up and, in truth, women are discounted at every turn.

Later, in my counseling practice, my weekly women's support groups, seminars, workshops and retreats many women came to me from similar backgrounds for help. The following story of one of those women will give a picture of the challenges faced by the women raised in that environment and those who are trying to help them.

Julie (not her real name) came to a retreat and was withdrawn, sat silently with her head bowed, wore no make up and said little. The retreat was limited to a group of 12 and by the third day she felt safe enough to speak up. She said she had been going to a counselor for help because of how she felt about herself and her fears about men. Her counselor had told her that she must have been sexually abused as a child because she was displaying all the classic symptoms.

Julie didn't remember any events of sexual abuse, but her counselor assured her that she must have blocked it out and insisted she think back to her father, uncles or brother to find the person who had done 'something' to her. She could think of nothing and asked her mother. Her mother was shocked and said nothing like that could have happened but the therapist insisted. Julie's father was considerably upset and became angry that such a suggestion could be made and the accusations upset the family which made life even more difficult for her.

When she related this at the retreat, Julie looked at the floor and said she had come to get some answers and didn't know what to think. She asked me if I would help her to remember who it could have been.

First I thanked her for her courage in sharing her story and agreed that it must be very confusing for her to have all these symptoms without the usual cause being evident. I asked her if I could ask a question and she said yes. I then asked her to describe the church she grew up in and the extent of her parents' involvement. I was not surprised when she said she was raised as one of Jehovah's Witnesses, her parents were still involved but she was not and they had not been close since she left the organization.

I have had well over 50 such people from a variety of extremely strict religious backgrounds come to my events with a similar story.

When a young girl is raised in a rules oriented, male dominated, women subjugated belief system she gets some very strong messages about who women are, who men are and what she must be as she grows up. Young girls get the message about who they are as a woman from their fathers. When a father praises his daughter and shows her he loves her she grows up with a good sense of who she is as a woman and how to relate to men in a healthy way.

However, when a young girl is raised seeing her mother being told she is not worthy, cannot hold any position of leadership, cannot even pray in front of her family and has no say in any decisions she gets a very different message about who she herself will be as a woman. She gets very clear messages about what women are and what their position is in relationship to men. As a result when she grows up and moves into womanhood she may demonstrate some of the following symptoms:

1. May believe that men are superior to her

2. May believe it is her place to make a man happy and that if he is not happy or something goes wrong in the relationship it must be her fault

3. May be attracted to men who are controlling, narcissistic and abusive emotionally, spiritually and/or physically

4. May never feel she measures up

5. Believes that she is stuck forever in this way of thinking and cannot make any changes

6. Accepts painful behavior from men (what they say or do) because she believes she is powerless against it and that it is okay for men to do this

7. Will have no personal power in the presence of a man

8. May find it difficult to express herself and will be nervous around men

9. Will be fearful when a man expresses disapproval or anger

10. May believe there is something wrong with her that cannot be fixed

11. Blames others for things that go wrong in her life

12. Has a 'victim' mentality – believes that nothing good will ever come to her and that her hopes and dreams are meaningless and will never be fulfilled

13. May stay in a job she hates because she doesn't think she deserves better

Many therapists are not aware that a girl growing up in any strict, fundamental church or religious belief will have these symptoms and will immediately think there has been some sexual abuse in childhood. I don't know if there has been very much in print on this dynamic, but I have seen it over and over in the work that I do. I have also seen families torn apart because the real reason for the problem is not identified.

Religious beliefs root very deeply in the psyche of children. Many adults who have not been inside a church since their teens will still identify themselves by the belief system their parents exposed them to an early age. It should be no surprise that parents who expose themselves and their children to belief systems that denigrate women and treat them as second-class citizens will raise daughters who struggle with their own identity as women.

I have had many women come through programs I've either taught or supervised who came from this kind of background and found their value through hard work and perseverance. One woman, in particular, came back to a group to report on her progress. She said she realized how to identify a controlling relationship. She said if I'm in it, it's controlling. I am pleased to say that woman did eventually come to know what a truly lovely woman she was, she found her value and created a healthy relationship and a fulfilling life.

Many times I'm asked how does one identify a controlling relationship or group, especially a church that may be leaning in that direction. We aren't always aware that we are being drawn into this kind of situation until it is too late. Some of us just know life isn't comfortable or happy, but we don't know what to do about it. Others have recognized it, but still aren't sure of the way to go. Let me assure you there is help, there are people who are interested and you do have choices. You always have choices.

The following are the two BIG questions I am frequently asked when I've spoken on this in the past.

1. How do I know if I am in a controlling relationship?

If you can identify any of the following symptoms in your relationship, you may want to consider there is a level of control that is not healthy and seek some help.

1. **Jekyll and Hyde personality** – he or she may get angry or even physically abusive and then become remorseful and show a very contrite and loving side. You tolerate the 'challenging' side of the personality and hope the 'nice' side will become permanent. But it never does and as much as you may not want to hear this, it never will. The 'nice' side will come out when it is needed to win you

back but it is the other side you will live with.

2. **May get angry for no reason** – anything or nothing can trigger an anger session. There will be an argument in which you will always be wrong and once you apologize and acquiesce things are fine again for a while.

3. **Must account for all your time** – going to the store, being with friends, or just leaving the house for a walk will all have time limits and you must account for any missing minutes. If you are out shopping or visiting there will be phone calls every so many minutes to see 'how you are', 'where you are', or 'when you will be back'. These calls and demands for time accounting may be under the guise of concern for your welfare, his or her love for you and/or your safety.

4. **May dictate what you wear or how you look** – May complain about some physical feature or insist you dress a certain way. May give 'back-handed' compliments such as "That dress looks so good, too bad you have a tummy."

5. **Handles all the money** – You have to ask for any spending money and have no say in financial decisions. You may not even know how much money is coming in or what the living expenses are. If you are given a weekly amount for yourself you may have to account for how it is spent.

6. **Confuse love and caring with control or domination** – You see the control or the lack of freedom as caring or being loved and looked after but it feels claustrophobic and suffocating at times. Any attempt to discuss this is either dismissed or triggers anger or you are made to feel guilty because the other person 'cares so much' about where you are, whom you are with or whom you are talking to on the phone.

7. **Discounts your desires, schedule or plans** -- Your plans always get sabotaged in some way. What the other person wants you to do becomes more important than what you want to do or have planned. You have to cancel things to favor the other person's desires or last minute requests.

8. **Your friends and family don't care for him/her or say you've changed** – Listen to your friends and your family. They love you and want the best for you. If they tell you you've changed in some way since this person has been in your life, listen to them and take what they say as a major warning. They are seeing things you are blind to or are choosing to ignore.

9. **You find yourself apologizing for his/her behavior** – You overlook him/her discounting or disrespecting you, your friends or family and/or using language or words that insult, contradict or humiliate you or them. If you find yourself saying, "You just don't know him/her like I do", you are in a controlling relationship that will be a big problem over time.

10. **Jealousy masked as caring or being concerned** – You are not permitted to speak with members of the opposite sex, even workmen at the house. In fact, workmen may not be permitted to come to your house unless your partner or spouse is at home. You cannot be alone with your friends or if you are there is a myriad of questions and/or accusations about your behavior. Past relationships

are brought up in arguments and held against you. You cannot have friends that have not been met and approved of by your partner.

11. **Fear that either you will leave or you will be left** – He or she is fearful you will leave and they will be alone. This deep insecurity will drive their controlling behaviors but is presented to you as deep-seated love and devotion. Or, you may be afraid you will be left because you are constantly told how 'lucky' you are to be with that person.

12. **You are blamed for anything that goes wrong** – It will be your fault if the other person loses their temper. No matter how any conversation starts out, a problem in any area of the relationship will be your fault.

13. **Fear for your physical safety** – This is a major red flag! If you have been physically hurt, or if you fear you may be, get help immediately. There are telephone hot-lines listed in phone books in most cities you can call and someone will give you help with what to do to protect yourself. Never stay in a

physically dangerous relationship. There is no such thing as a 'minor incident' in a relationship.

2. How do you identify a controlling church or religion?

Again, these are some of the symptoms you will see in a controlling church or a cult. If you can identify any of these in the group you belong to, you may want to consider talking to someone, getting help and leaving.

1. **Claim to be special** – to have 'The Truth' or some special insight or teaching that no one else has.

2. **Authoritarian or Dictatorial** – People are told what to believe or to think and cannot come to their own conclusions or insights. They must agree with the leadership or be shamed or humiliated in some way.

3. **'We vs. They' mentality** – The special status invites claims of persecution and the need to be separate or protected from anyone outside of the church or organization. Outsiders are considered a

threat because they question and challenge the unique beliefs and could weaken someone's 'faith'.

4. **Predicting dates or prophecies about the future** – A date or time frame will be given when some catastrophe will hit everyone except this particular group. This group will be spared, but everyone else on the planet will be destroyed or will miss out on some blessing because they haven't listened to the group leadership or agreed with the beliefs. The dates predicted will come and go with excuses as to why the prophecies did not happen as predicted or a 'spiritual' explanation will be given of something happening that no one could see physically.

5. **Discipline and/or punishment for perceived 'wrong doing'** – when someone breaks a rule or questions authority there is some kind of singling out publicly or privately and some form of discipline administered through either verbal reproof, limiting interaction with other members or even loss of hope for eternity.

6. **Work, work, and more work** – there is a demand for constant activity toward the group or organization. Either teaching, cleaning or working in some other capacity all for the benefit of the organization and to the expense physically and financially of the membership.

7. **No outside information allowed** – members or followers in the group are not allowed to read outside information such as books, magazines or even leaflets or pamphlets printed by other organizations. Nor can members watch any TV, films or programs not approved by the leadership.

8. **Strict discipline of children is expected and endorsed** – Unreasonable demands will be put on children to sit still for long periods or be punished for infractions of rules. There is pressure on parents to always keep children 'in line'. Some religious groups will even have a 'spanking room' in the back. Children are not encouraged to speak up or to express opinions or views unless it is to 'parrot' the organizations doctrines or beliefs.

9. **Legalistic thinking** – there are many rules to be followed and consequences if they aren't. Rules are more important than relationships. If someone is being punished or disciplined even family members and close friends must abide by the rules surrounding the discipline. Parents may even have to withdraw from their children of any age providing only food and necessities for the duration of the punishment.

10. **Special Language** – different words for common beliefs or items that set the followers apart from outsiders. Phrases and/or terms that are recognized by the group but not outsiders give exclusivity to members and a 'coded' language.

(See also "Toxic Faith" by Stephen Arterburn and Jack Felton published by Oliver Nelson, a Division of Thomas Nelson Publishers)

Whether you are looking at the first or second list, if you can identify only two or three of the things mentioned you are in a relationship with a person or an organization that needs your concerned attention. Most people who can identify two or three things on either list are blind to any other things they may be able to identify because protecting the person or organization is paramount.

If you can identify anything on these lists as happening in your relationship or the organization governing your belief system, it is imperative that you sit down with someone who knows you well, loves and cares about you and has already expressed concern about your welfare in your situation. Ask them to read these lists with you and help you to identify anything you may be missing or overlooking.

How to help yourself after leaving a controlling relationship

Leaving a cult, or any controlling relationship presents challenges, but I assure you those challenges can be overcome. It is important to keep in mind that you cannot change the other person or the organization and you cannot rescue them. No matter how much you care for the controlling person or for your friends in a controlling organization the very best thing you can do for yourself is to refuse to be their victim any longer.

If you are leaving a controlling relationship you may think you can encourage the controlling person to get professional help, but if you do, don't expect your encouragement to be well received. Your compassion may not be understood or welcomed and could be used against you. In my own experience and talking with others who have had similar experiences, the following things were found to be the most helpful in moving toward a life of peace, happiness and enjoyment. This is by no means the complete list, but will hopefully give you a starting place to rebuild your life to be one of love, laughter and fulfillment.

1. Meet new people

The biggest challenge is realizing there are people outside the organization or outside of the relationship who are good and will enjoy your company as you get to know and enjoy them. There are many places to do this. First of all, write down all the names of people you can think of who were not part of the group you have left. As you look at that list, next to each name write down what you admire about that person. Now, look again and see if there is anyone on that list you can trust enough to call on the phone or visit briefly to begin to build a friendship.

You may find cards or flyers posted in bookstores for reading clubs in your area. Perhaps going to the library, local museums or schools of any level when there are speakers or presentations on something that interests you. That's a good way to meet people who have interests similar to your own. You can also look at www.meetup.com online and find meetings in your area of people who are interested in the same things you are. It's another great way to meet new people, make new friends, and begin to realize you have value to yourself and others.

2. Be with people who celebrate you, not those who tolerate you

When we have been in a controlling relationship we are used to being around people who tell us when we are wrong, or what's wrong with us. We are not used to compliments and don't know ourselves what we are good at or enjoy. If we do think we know, we constantly apologize for it or we dismiss ourselves, believing it's wrong to credit us with anything. We have become used to following someone else's likes or dislikes, their concepts of right and wrong, their rules, their hopes, dreams and desires.

We've done this for so long we've forgotten what we want, what we are good at, what we enjoy, dream about or desire out of life. In other words, we are used to being tolerated in someone else's world. Now is the time to learn it is okay to be celebrated in our own world. It's okay to hear compliments and simply say "Thank you" and not dismiss someone's gift of gracious words that speak into our soul and fill our heart. Be around those people who appreciate you and who enjoy being with you and the person you are.

You can tell when you are around someone who loves you and celebrates you, because when you are around that person you like who you are. A good friend helps you to be the very best 'you' you can be. If you are with someone who makes you feel badly about yourself, flee! Get away from that person and be with the ones who will encourage, empower and celebrate you.

3. Keep your support system (or build one)

You may have been cut off from friends and family who love you and who support you, but now is the time to turn to them and let them know you need their love and support. You need people to turn to. This is the time to identify those people who you were close to at one time but have been separated from because of the relationship or the controlling organization you've been involved with. I've seen time and again these people are more than happy to rekindle the relationship and help you make positive steps forward. Rather than judge you for what happened, they will most often be supportive and happy for you and will encourage you in your bold step to freedom.

4. Avoid judgmental people (including your own judgmental thoughts)

People have been very quick to tell us what we 'should' think, feel or believe. We are so used to living by someone else's standards that even though they are not around, their voices are in our heads and our unconscious thoughts. Sometimes we live our lives by the voices of our parents, perhaps a controlling spouse or the leadership of a controlling, cultic group. No matter where those voices come from, now is the time to begin to deal with them and put them into perspective.

Because of our history with controlling people and their messages, we have the people who are constantly in judgment of us on a pedestal and those voices speak much louder than our own. Here is a simple exercise to put those voices into perspective. First, think of the person who has given you the most judgmental messages. That's the voice that always speaks in your head whenever you want to do or think something differently from them. It's the voice that tells you why you will fail, or why you don't deserve good things in your life. It's the voice that tells you happiness is for others but not for you.

Now, picture that person in your mind standing on a very high chair. Over time you've been put into a very childish place around that person so that you are always looking up, always feeling down and never feeling equal. Now, muster your courage and in your mind, take that person off the chair and stand so that you are eye to eye. What would you like to tell that person? Go ahead! Say it now. How does that feel?

Only very insecure people want to control you. People who are secure in themselves are happy for you to be you and to meet you eye to eye. Now is the time to learn that everyone has opinions and ideas. Everyone has their own desires, longings, hopes and dreams. No one has the 'right' desires, longings, hopes and dreams. We have what we have and ours will be different from someone else's and that's okay! Your desires, hopes and dreams deserve to be honored as much as another person's.

You don't have to remain with people who are constantly in judgment of you. If it is a parent or a relative and you cannot completely walk away from the person, set some guidelines around what you are willing to discuss or not discuss. How long are you willing to hold a conversation with that person? What can you say when their judgment of you starts? Find a way to be polite and yet leave the scene or change the subject when you begin to feel unequal.

5. Don't assume you should get along with everyone

I'm often asked how to get along with difficult people. My reply has always been that unless you are related to them or working for them, why would you want to? If we have a history of being controlled in some way, we may believe that we should be able to get along with everyone and if we don't it is our fault. Here's a silver bullet of truth for you, "You won't get along with everyone". Some people don't want to get along with you or anyone. Some people like to stir things up and some are so wounded they only know how to wound other people to feel good about themselves.

It isn't your job to fix everyone on the planet. It is your job to make good contributions into the lives of other people and to accept their good contributions into your life. You also have permission to reject their painful contributions and not accept them and it is okay to do this.

If you find you are around someone you simply don't get on with, why continually put yourself in that situation. It's okay for you to decide who your friends are. We are so used to being in a melting pot of personalities inside a controlled group or relationship we forget we can make choices about who we will or won't associate with.

6. Stay away from other people's 'small boxes' of thinking

Upon leaving a cult, well-meaning people will immediately tell you what you 'should' think or believe now that you are out of the organization. You may be bombarded by people who are concerned that you now believe what they say are the 'right' things. In other words, people will want you to believe what they believe. You have just escaped a very small box of thinking and control. Be very careful you don't enter someone else's small box of thinking and control.

Allow yourself time to explore ideas, beliefs, and all the wonderful things now available to you to choose from. You have the freedom to make your own decisions about what you want to think or believe, about what belief system or group you want to be part of. You also have the freedom to choose no organized group or way of thinking.

Our cultural norm is to belong to something that is culturally acceptable. But you now have the freedom to question everything and everyone. Explore, examine, research and enjoy the journey of discovering what is right for 'YOU'! You are on your own pathway, not someone else's. Be free to explore what your life is all about, who you are, and what pathway feels right for you.

7. Explore for yourself what you feel comfortable with spiritually
One of the most difficult adjustments upon coming out of a cult is the realization that you have the freedom to explore different belief systems, philosophies, paradigms, cultures and religions. You have the freedom to choose which is right for you, or none at all. You have emerged from a group where you were told what to think and what to believe. Your choices for exploration were taken from you and now you have them back. Now you have the freedom to choose which course, which direction, which path is best for you.

8. Find a mentor

You may feel completely alone and 'out to sea' with your newfound freedom and it can be a bit frightening. There are many who will step in and offer to guide you or mentor you. However, the person who steps forward to offer to be your mentor is usually someone who will want to direct you in their way and guide you into their own way of thinking. Eventually you will find yourself wanting to please that person and not yourself and you will be back under the same controls you've escaped although in a different form.

Look at the people around you who are living the kind of life and enjoying the kind of freedom to think that you want to enjoy yourself. That's the person to ask to mentor you. Know what it is that you want that person to do for you. It may be as simple as giving you permission to make your own decisions. It may be as in depth as asking that person to guide you through different areas of your life and help you to learn to make good choices.

Keep in mind, a good mentor is one who will help you find your own path and not attempt to put you on theirs.

9. Make small decisions first

Life can feel very overwhelming when you come out of any controlling relationship. You now have freedom, but you also have responsibility. This responsibility can feel quite heavy and confusing unless you learn how to carry it wisely.

There may be a desire to change everything in your life at once, but start with the small things. What do you want to do on a weekly basis just for yourself? How do you want to start and end your day? What do you truly like and enjoy and how can you bring that into your life. As you make small decisions and choices each day, it becomes easier and more realistic to take on the larger choices of career, residence and relationships.

10. Find a good therapist or help from someone who has had a similar experience

Never be afraid to get professional help if you see a need. There are many good therapists that can help you to take the steps you need to examine your thinking and to move into your new life of freedom in a responsible way. If you cannot afford therapy, or cannot find someone with whom you are comfortable, look for others who have had a similar experience to yours and who are making their life work well. Perhaps that person is not willing to be a mentor, but is willing to be a friend. Such a person, or friend, can understand what you are experiencing and can identify with your fears in a way that will allow you to talk to them and can listen with no judgment being passed.

11. Find a way to give to others

Pouring into others in some way is the best way to appreciate your new life and what you've learned from your experience. First look at those who around you who you care about, friends, neighbors, co-workers or relatives. Perhaps you can do small things such as sending a card, making a phone call or paying a compliment. Then look at ways to contribute into the community. Reading to children in a library, helping the elderly, volunteering for a soup kitchen or charity shop, giving food or offering a listening ear to a homeless person, are some great ways to pour into the lives of others.

This kind of contribution into the lives of other people helps to fill the heart of the giver. This kind of giving isn't because you 'have to', it's because you 'get to'. It's not work, it's a privilege. It doesn't take money to give love to another; it takes a heart that cares. When you care for others and fill their hearts, your own heart fills and your appreciation for your own life will deepen.

12. Learn to 'play'

Life is not all about work. Coming from a controlling organization or relationship we feel like we must be 'busy' at all times and life is serious. There isn't much time for relaxing, reading a good book in front of the fire or laughing with friends in the middle of the day. Learn to enjoy your life and have fun with your children, your family and your friends. It's okay not to work 24/7. Enjoy the journey of your life every day.

13. Be grateful for the benefits of your experience

Every experience in life, no matter how painful, has benefits that must be recognized and appreciated if we are to move forward with love and joy. This balance exists in every experience, every interaction and every situation. Take the time to write down the benefits you gained from being part of the organization or relationship you have now left.

What did you learn? Before you say 'nothing', think about this very seriously. Those who take the time to do this hard work are enjoying a life of love, laughter and appreciation. Those who do not take the time to do this find themselves unhappy, feeling victimized, negative in their approach to new things and fearful of new people and opportunities. When you can be grateful for every experience, appreciate what you learned from them and recognize the benefits they have brought to your life you will be living a life of gratitude which will produce love and appreciation on a daily basis.

14. Enjoy life

Have fun! Go to the gym, take care of yourself physically, buy a new wardrobe, explore new things, enjoy lunch with friends, get exercise, breath in life and enjoy each day and all it has to offer.

You are free to explore who you are, what you like and dislike, how you want to dress or wear your hair and to ask questions of other people to find out what others are thinking. You have the freedom to hear their thoughts, beliefs, hopes and dreams and not have to argue them into the 'right' way to think or believe. Learn to appreciate their differences and individuality.

Every one has the right to enjoy their life and to experience the fullness of all it has to offer – especially you!

You are a magnificent creation of God with unlimited possibilities in an endless Universe of ideas, contemplations, philosophies, explorations and growth opportunities for your mind and Spirit. Learn to appreciate the magnificent gift you have received of a life that is unique to you as you contribute into the lives of others and allow your own heart to be filled with love.

What has helped former members of controlling organizations and relationships to rebuild their lives and regain their personal authority?

Here are the comments from some who were formerly involved with Jehovah's Witnesses or other types of controlling relationships. Some comments have been modified and names are not included to protect their privacy.

"The main thing I did was stay focused on the reasons why I left. I also listened to experiences online of others who had the courage to leave. And I would constantly read up on the organization's interpretations of 'truth' and use my own logic to sort through and see for myself. I had a very supportive family when I first came out, but as soon as I stopped going to church with them, their support vanished. Since I knew I was doing the right thing for me, my conscious was clear and I didn't need anyone else's approval." A.S.

"When I first left I really didn't believe I

deserved to be lifted up. I believed the gutter was where I belonged and I got involved in drugs and sex and became homeless, although I didn't quit school. I eventually found, with the help of a couple of good friends, what love is and started to surround myself with like minds. I took in whatever knowledge of God I could. For me it was taking in different views of everything that did it. I asked a LOT of Questions." E.C.

"I used to walk into bookstores, and tell myself I could buy the book that 'speaks to me' the loudest. So I read a lot of self-help books, Sufi poetry, Buddhist meditations, and Hinduism. Many of the messages contained in those books really made a lot of sense, and assisted me spiritually. Also, it helps to have at least one friend that you can be totally honest with, when life is up or down. I love to travel, and I am fascinated by other religions, cultures and places." S.M.

"I really had to put into practice what I was taught at home, and to let go of my 'need' to be accepted. I had to learn to love myself and so, going inward was very important --

listening to my "inner voice". In short, I needed to find myself and heal from all the dysfunction in my life." D.V.

"I spent three years in therapy, lost almost 200 pounds, got my GED, had a few different jobs, spent 5 years smoking weed and writing my thoughts and feelings down. I journaled and wrote poetry and talked to anyone who would listen about what was going on with the JW's and my life." L.J.

"The thing that really helped was good Christian fellowship. Our church has potlucks every other Sunday and after service we eat together and it brings us closer as a family. I've lost all of my extended family so my church is the only family I have ever had and it's those friendships that help fill the gaps". A.A.

"It was and still is a slow process. I did meticulous research in the Bible, history and archeology. I went through a lot of emotional turmoil realizing how the Watchtower and their Bible translation was all about lies and

manipulation. I came to the same conclusion as that of Bart Ehrman, the Bible scholar. I found we do not have any of the original scriptures, that Bible books were written sometimes a hundred years or more after the supposed author died. I love 'truth' and what I found was traumatic. My conclusion is that truth is all about love, respect, compassion, helping anyone when possible and not being judgmental. I believe that we are here to learn, evolve and gain knowledge. It is up to each one of us to find the meaning of our life. Trust your intuition and your instinct, many people love you. This will give you the strength to grow and have inner peace."
R.B.

"I read a lot of self help books and tried to educate myself. I got my instructor's license to do hair and was going to become a flight attendant. I loved to dance and went out dancing a lot, which helped me keep in shape. I was just sooo glad I was free of the oppression I was raised with. I wanted to build my self-esteem. I did not leave JW until I was 35, so most things were deeply engrained. After leaving I made lots of friends and traveled." S.G.

"I think it is important to keep busy, to help people and to distance oneself from the tendency for self pity. Encourage friendships with people you trust. Talk to rational ex-JW's. I also believe it is important to start at the very beginning to find out what 'you' really believe. There are a number of good books that will help you from authors who use facts." R.K.

"By the time I left I was doing fine emotionally. What I felt I needed was to research, find answers and critically examine everything so that I never fall for a scam like the Witnesses again." R.O.

"Make new friends and get as far away from the WT as possible, whether you pursue religion or not." R.W.

"I was thrilled to be out. I remember waking up on Saturday knowing I didn't have to go door-to-door. Then I slept in on Sunday. My suggestion to anyone leaving is to fill that

time otherwise spent in the W.T. with hobbies and socializing with good quality friends. The biggest thing is to get good friends, socialize, go out and do new things. Spend time reading up on cults and behavior control." N.B.

"I've never been a Witness but I was in a violent relationship and to cut a long story short I stood up to him and left. Now I'm free, confident and happy. It's been six years and he still tries to manipulate me but I have the strength now to stand up to him. In effect, this is what religious organizations do to you when they control and manipulate you." K.J.

"I do yoga, read, write my thoughts and spend more time focused on the future than behind me, pray, smile with my kids, and sometimes tune it all out with a glass of wine and something frivolous. I always think to myself, who do I want to be at the end of my life? When I look back I hope my triumphs will outweigh my regrets. I keep an open mind that I don't have all the answers and neither do my friends. It's good to

emotionally back off sometimes from the ex J's even if you are still helping. There's a cauldron of ideology in it that can pull you off your own path. Just always be sure to remind yourself who YOU are." E.N.

And last, but by far not least is a message from Barbara Radke, my friend who was one of a large group who encouraged me to write this book. She wrote:

What I needed to build myself up after leaving the WT....

Let's start with my thoughts here ~~

- ❖ *After "researching" the word "Inspired" in Watchtower literature*
- ❖ *After listening to your "Legalism to Love" talk on a website and contacting you*
- ❖ *After reading what other JW's had to say on that site*
- ❖ *After reading Ray Franz's book, 'Crisis Of Conscience'*
- ❖ *After reflecting on the past 25 years on my personal experience within the Watchtower organization and upon seeing how others*

were 'handled' and 'dealt with'

❖ *After receiving a disturbing call from a JW elder*

…I decided enough was enough and I sent a 'goodbye' letter that evening.

I KNOW my mental health was being affected by it all. This was NOT a healthy environment to be in and these people were NOT my family. After hanging up the phone from talking briefly with the elder my nerves were so bad my hands started to 'quiver'. Eight months later the elder decided to make return visits to my husband after no one came to visit him for five years. My hands still shook for an entire year with each of his visits. I wondered why. What was I lacking that my soul needed?

Empowerment? Yes, there was a 'hole in my soul' so to speak that needed to be healed. My heart was stricken with grief and my mind was not at rest. Now, I no longer grieve, and I am at rest. No one knows what the future holds from day to day but when we have today we have life and leaving the WT gives us the freedom to enjoy it to the max.

When I first left the WT organization, someone mentioned the word 'legalism' to me. I had no idea what she was talking about. I knew the laws of the land were to be followed but 'legalism' in a religious sense was foreign to me. And then I realized I had lived this legalistic way for 25 years. How blind was that?

Religious legalism is, as I've found, when regulations replace relationship, when performance for the WT replaces passion and love for God with rules, the 'do's and don'ts' demand obedience or else there is punishment.

Love is not enforced in any way in life but I find it's the most powerful 'tool' anyone could possess to help another along life's journey. I'd rather stand behind someone who loves me than stand behind someone who wanted to control me with a whip or a fist." Barb Radke

CPSIA information can be obtained at www.ICGtesting.com
Printed in the USA
LVOW101548130312

272907LV00011B/56/P

9 781936 944002